Cambridge Elements ≡

Elements in Politics and Society in Latin America
edited by
Maria Victoria Murillo
Columbia University
Tulia G. Falleti
University of Pennsylvania
Juan Pablo Luna
The Pontifical Catholic University of Chile
Andrew Schrank
Brown University

THE CIRCUIT OF DETACHMENT IN CHILE

Understanding the Fate of a Neoliberal Laboratory

Kathya Araujo
Universidad de Santiago de Chile

CAMBRIDGE
UNIVERSITY PRESS

Shaftesbury Road, Cambridge CB2 8EA, United Kingdom

One Liberty Plaza, 20th Floor, New York, NY 10006, USA

477 Williamstown Road, Port Melbourne, VIC 3207, Australia

314–321, 3rd Floor, Plot 3, Splendor Forum, Jasola District Centre, New Delhi – 110025, India

103 Penang Road, #05–06/07, Visioncrest Commercial, Singapore 238467

Cambridge University Press is part of Cambridge University Press & Assessment, a department of the University of Cambridge.

We share the University's mission to contribute to society through the pursuit of education, learning and research at the highest international levels of excellence.

www.cambridge.org
Information on this title: www.cambridge.org/9781009310710

DOI: 10.1017/9781009310697

First published 2022

A catalogue record for this publication is available from the British Library.

ISBN 978-1-009-31071-0 Paperback
ISSN 2515-5253 (online)
ISSN 2515-5245 (print)

Cambridge University Press & Assessment has no responsibility for the persistence or accuracy of URLs for external or third-party internet websites referred to in this publication and does not guarantee that any content on such websites is, or will remain, accurate or appropriate.

The Circuit of Detachment in Chile

Understanding the Fate of a Neoliberal Laboratory

Elements in Politics and Society in Latin America

DOI: 10.1017/9781009310697
First published online: August 2022

Kathya Araujo
Universidad de Santiago de Chile
Author for correspondence: Kathya Araujo, kathya.araujo@gmail.com

Abstract: This Element discusses the consequences for the social bond of the conjoint action of the economic and social model inspired by the premises of neoliberalism and of the powerful pressures for the democratization of social relations in Chilean society. It is based upon empirical research developed in the past twenty years. The main argument in this Element is that these processes have had as one of their most important effects the generation of a circuit of detachment, that is, a process that leads to different forms of disidentification and distancing from logics and principles that govern social relations and interaction. It is a dynamic circuit consisting of four components: excess, disenchantment, irritation, and, finally, detachment. The Element analyzes this circuit and each of its components as well as its consequences for the social bond. It also includes a brief reflection on the impact of this circuit on the political bond.

Keywords: neoliberalism, social democratization, social bond, political bond, Chile

ISBNs: 9781009310710 (PB), 9781009310697 (OC)
ISSNs: 2515-5253 (online), 2515-5245 (print)

Contents

1 Introduction

1.1 A Thesis

This Element addresses a specific set of concerns: the effects on individuals and societies of our current historical condition, one strongly shaped by the adoption and expansion of the so-called neoliberal economic and social model.[1] The Element explores the consequences of this model for societal bonds and for the political future of our societies. It does so by examining the case of Chile, a country considered the first laboratory of neoliberalism due to the country's early adoption of the neoliberal model. Chile, however, is also considered a particularly radical case of neoliberalism because the country's adoption of neoliberal policies and of institutional features designed to ensure the continuity of these policies occurred under a dictatorial regime, that of Augusto Pinochet (1973–90).

In the course of research carried out over the past twenty years, I have found that Chileans perceive their country to have undergone a genuine historical change. This perception is not an abstract judgment on their part but, rather, a result of their lived experience, of having to face challenges in ordinary life for which the social "know-how" they possessed no longer seemed to work. Thus, Chileans have participated in a major and unforeseen way in transformations not only of society but also of individuals themselves and of how relationships between them are organized.

My research findings also indicate a second factor that has reshaped social life in Chile in recent decades, namely pressures for the democratization of social relations (Araujo and Martuccelli 2012).

The establishment – via institutional changes, the adoption of laws, and normative principles and via changes in the social imaginaries – of an economic and social model inspired by the premises of neoliberalism placed new structural demands on individuals. These changes radically transformed the challenges individuals had to face in their social lives – for example, in their working lives and in their ways of coping with retirement and aging or with the new rules set for them as economic subjects – at the same time as they promoted new social ideals (e.g., competition, flexibility, or new social status indicators). As a result of the ongoing experience of having to face the demands of social life with little help from the state, relying basically on themselves (or, at most, on family or friends), Chileans have developed a strong sense of feeling overwhelmed but they have also developed greater confidence in their abilities

---

[1] A discussion of the term neoliberalism and the shape it takes in Chile is fully developed in Section 2.

and capacities to face the challenges of social life on their own while distancing themselves from institutions. They have acquired a new understanding of what being socially worthy entails (e.g., being a consumer, a proprietor, etc.) and a new definition of the minimum of revenues that can be expected from society.

On the other hand, powerful pressures for the democratization of social relations, understood as the spread of normative ideals (such as law, equality, autonomy, or diversity) to ever more spheres of social relations (male–female and child–adult relations, among others), transformed perceptions, demands, and moral judgments concerning the individuals themselves and their relationship with society. These ideals created new expectations of how individuals should be treated by institutions and by others, prompting individuals to conceive of themselves in new ways, and provided new tools for evaluating society. These ideals prompted new expectations of horizontality and added urgency to a renewal of the principles that regulate relationships and interpersonal interactions (for example, new expectations about the rules of deference to authority figures).

All of the above has led to a period of contention. This conflict has, of course, political expressions, such as the Chilean social outburst of October 2019,[2] but, as I will argue below, these are just the tip of the iceberg. What lies at the core of these disputes is that Chilean society currently consists of transformed individuals engaged in a tense, exhausting, conflictive, and ambivalent rearticulation of the logics and principles that order social relations and interactions.

My main argument in this Element is that one of the most important effects of Chileans' journey in recent decades has been the generation of *a circuit of detachment*; that is, the generation of a process that leads to different forms of disidentification and distancing from institutions and from the social logics and principles that order the social bond. This is a dynamic process comprising four components: excessiveness, disenchantment, irritation, and, finally, detachment.

---

[2] The demonstrations began in October 2019, with October 18th typically considered the symbolic start date. The demonstrations continued, although on a significantly smaller scale, until the summer of 2020. The coronavirus pandemic that struck Chile in March 2020 interrupted the mobilization but did not cause it to disappear. Protests have continued to occur sporadically, involving more limited groups of people. The protest outbreak of 2019 far exceeded previous levels of conflict observed in Chile. According to Joignant et al. (2020), the baseline level of adversarial activity in Chile at the time was around 500 protests per semester. Between October 18 and December 31, 2019, 2,700 adversarial events were recorded, 40 percent of them involving the use of violence. The events had a powerful social and political impact, leading the government to promise a referendum on whether to change the constitution dictated in 1980 under the Pinochet dictatorship, an option that was approved by 78.28 percent of voters. Debate over the crafting of a new constitution figured prominently in the contentious presidential elections of 2021 and the fate and consequences of these political disputes are part of a story that is still unfolding.

Excessiveness is linked to the experience of facing immoderate structural exigencies or demands, such as uncertainty, that incessantly impel one to action. It is also associated with the perception of being constantly overwhelmed by demands and under pressure. Both are very often experienced as a breach of one's limits (physical, health, motivational, psychic, etc.).

Disenchantment is the effect of broken promises. It emerges from the experience of a conflict between, on the one hand, the promises of neoliberalism and democratization and, on the other, the realities of ordinary social life. Disenchantment gives rise to distrust but also to a very skeptical view of the social world and its institutions and actors.

Irritation refers to a hypersensitivity and disproportionality between stimulus and response that characterizes interactions and relations between individuals and between individuals and institutions. Irritation is at odds with civility and is related to the fact that social relations and interactions are seen and experienced as charged with friction, mostly tinged with anger, and dominated by a noticeable deregulation of the use of force.

Detachment, the last component, denotes an irregular and complex process of estrangement and disengagement from the principles, rationalities, and legitimacies that order the social bond, without complete abandonment of society. Links that bind us to society and to a shared life are loosened and customary ways of relating to one another and to institutions lose effectiveness. Detachment is an individual self-protective response to the harshness of social life.

This circuit can be understood to operate diachronically, such that excessiveness is followed by disenchantment, disenchantment by irritation, and irritation by detachment. But these elements can also be seen to operate synchronically, such that they are simultaneously active and provide feedback to one another.

This circuit has important social consequences, as I will discuss below, and also incurs risks to the political bond. As my work has shown, individuals' assessment of democracy is not limited to their evaluation of the functioning of its institutions. Rather, democracy is a living entity. While its existence and solidity depend on the relationships that individuals establish with the normative principles and the set of promises of which democracy is constituted, these relationships depend, in turn, on the social experiences with which individuals are confronted and on how these experiences affect individuals' trust in and adherence to democracy, its institutions, and its actors. As I have found, experiences such as the use of personal connections to get a job or of being treated in daily interactions as of lesser value than those who are richer, whiter, or possessed a prestigious family name strongly erode the political bond. Everyday social experiences are, crucially, the proving ground on which people's adherence and fidelity to democracy will depend (Araujo 2017). Thus, the political bond is strongly influenced by the vicissitudes of the social bond. The circuit of detachment, given its centrifugal motion – that is, the fact that it is moved by an outward force, which pushes individuals away from the center toward the margins of society – establishes a set of very serious political challenges.

1.2 A Thesis in Context

The question of how structural changes in recent decades have affected Chilean society and individuals is not a new issue. For example, the second half of the 1990s witnessed a fierce debate between those who emphasized the advantages of modernization (Brunner 1992) and rated it a success and those who espoused more critical perspectives. The term *modernization* refers to the effects of the economic and societal model first implemented under the military dictatorship of Augusto Pinochet and then continued, without fundamental changes, under the center-left Coalition of Parties for Democracy (Garretón 2012) that ruled the country without interruption from 1990 to 2010. In this debate, three major critical diagnoses were advanced, each emphasizing a particular theme: 1) exploitation and alienation (Moulian 1997; 1998); 2) malaise (United Nations Development Programme, PNUD 1998, 2002; Lechner 1990, 2006); and 3) the rupture or weakening of collective identity and community values (Bengoa 1996; Larrraín 2001; Tironi 1999).

This discussion entered a new phase around the first half of the 2010s, sparked by some fresh developments. The defenders of modernization continued to interpret the vicissitudes of Chilean society as predictable effects of the modernization process. They emphasized Chileans' high level of satisfaction with society and denied that modernization was the cause of social ills (Guzmán and Oppliger 2012; Gonzáles 2017). On the other hand, the critical perspective on modernization increasingly developed, implicitly or explicitly, under the influence of the student movement[3] and, more generally, under the influence of a new cycle of social mobilization (Somma 2017), which saw its greatest expression in the sequence of events culminating in the protests of

---

[3] The 2006 student movement, known as the "penguin revolution" and involving secondary school students, first centered on protests against the increase in the cost of the University Selection Test and for a reduction in public transport fares. It ended with demands for the repeal of the Organic Constitutional Law of Education, the reversal of the municipalization of schools, and the reinstatement of free education, all of which had unprecedented public support. The 2011 mobilization, by contrast, had university students as its main protagonists and even greater social outreach and public support. Its demands included an end to profitmaking, a questioning of the neoliberal economic growth model, discontent with student debt, and demands for a quality public education (Ruiz 2020: 70–71).

October 2019. What had been a discussion regarding the more generic question of modernization became a specific debate about the consequences of neoliberalism. The critics' formerly pessimistic tone gave way to a more optimistic outlook, strongly influenced by the increase and success of political mobilizations. Although criticism of neoliberalism and consumerism generally continued, alongside the criticism there emerged an epic discourse on individuals as political actors (Ruiz and Boccardo 2015; Mayol 2013; PNUD 2015).

The thesis of the circuit of detachment shares with prior critical contributions the diagnosis that the structural changes to Chilean society over the past several decades have produced an important set of consequences, both for individuals and for social life. However, there are at least four major differences between what previous authors have proposed and what my research has suggested.

First, there is a difference in the weight given to political factors and political junctures when explaining social change. The research I have conducted reveals that the social processes discussed are of long duration and cannot be reduced to political junctures, nor can they be understood solely in political terms. Protest and mobilization phenomena, no matter how significant, are not self-referential. My thesis focuses on social processes and dynamics that crystallize over a long period and that, I argue, take precedence over political explanations.

Second, prior contributions generally have emphasized a single structural explanatory dimension, the economic one, and have posited neoliberalism as the main explanatory factor. My research, as I have argued, reveals the centrality of a second factor – namely, pressure for the democratization of social relations. Interpretations of Chile that fail to consider the complex relationship between the two factors paint an inaccurate and misleading picture of the country.

Third, my findings suggest that Chile's structural transformations are much more ambivalent in nature. Some examples, to which we will return later, may help clarify the point. If discontent with the "model" or the "system" appears to be widespread, it is nevertheless true that the evidence shows that Chileans do not altogether reject the societal changes they have undergone (Araujo and Martuccelli 2012: Vol. I, 29–80). While it is true that there is an increase in individualism, in the sense of an affirmation of individualities, this is not necessarily perceived or experienced as anomic or threatening, as many of the studies reviewed assume. Such a development is a precondition for the affirmation of autonomy in a society that has long favored tutelary forms of hierarchy management (Araujo 2016). Attitudes toward the concept of merit provide another example. The merit linked to meritocracy has been seen by many academics (Sandel 2020; Khan 2011) as associated with the intensity with which the logic of the market is structured and installed in societies, and, therefore, as a formula for the maintenance of privileges and reproduction of inequalities. However, my findings have shown that, in the case of Chile, merit is seen as an essential component of the sense of justice and as a tool for defending the principle of equality because it plays an key role in breaking the historical logic of privilege that has permeated social relations in Chilean society and in other Latin America countries (Araujo and Martuccelli 2012).

Fourth, compared with prior work, my thesis takes a more nuanced view in interpreting both the neoliberal character of individuals in Chilean society and the opposite, idealized, epic-political characterization of them. My studies, for example, reveal the presence of individuals who might be called *relational hyper-actors* (Araujo and Martuccelli 2014), individuals who are placed in a difficult and even tragic relationship with the social values (such as competition) and the type of subjects that they are driven to embody, but who are simultaneously active in reproducing these ideal subject models. These persons have strong individual identities and reject selfishness but have serious difficulties committing to long-term relationships. They are highly sensitive to others' abuse of power but are themselves practiced in the use and confrontational mobilization of the power that they have at their disposal (whether real or virtual) as a relational logic.

In short, what distinguishes the thesis of the circuit of detachment is that it 1) gives analytical preeminence to the societal dimension; 2) employs a multifactorial approach to understanding Chile's historical situation by incorporating the dimension of the social bond; 3) takes a more ambivalent view of the effects of social change; and 4) views individuals in a way that neither idealizes nor demonizes them.

1.3 The Making of a Thesis

The development of this thesis and the arguments supporting it are based on the results of a series of eight large empirical studies carried out over the last twenty years.[4] Therefore, this Element is based upon a large body of work. While each of these studies explores specific topics (e.g., individuation, structural challenges, the exercise of authority, individuals' efforts to cope with social life, etc.), they share a common concern with the forms that the individual and the social bond take in the context of the structural changes that Chilean society has undergone in recent decades. In addition, all these studies share a common analytical framework.

---

[4] The different empirical studies that make up this research agenda are described in the Appendix accompanying this text. These research studies (henceforth "Inv. ") are numbered according to the order in which they were carried out.

To understand the effects of structural transformations on Chilean society and on the individuals who compose it, I have taken inspiration from the sociology of individuation (Martuccelli and de Singly 2018; Martuccelli 2006; Elias 2000) and have focused at the level of individuals. In my work,[5] I have approached the type of structural challenges they must face on a day-to-day basis, the strategies they employ to cope with these challenges, and the way in which these challenges and coping strategies influence the type of individuals they become. I have also paid close attention to the types of relationship they establish with the society in which they live. To address the latter, I have taken inspiration from studies of the social bond, that is, from a perspective that considers both the problem of social adherence (Bouvier 2005; Paugam 2017) and the outputs and inputs that a group mobilizes to shape the relationships and interactions between individuals (Goffman 1959).

This shared concern and shared analytical framework have shaped the research questions, defined the methodological inputs, and established the analytical procedures in each of the different studies carried out. This has enabled the results of each study to provide input for the subsequent research and allows each to be seen as a link in a chain of reasoning.

———

In what follows, I will present and discuss in detail the four components of the circuit of detachment: excessiveness (Section 2), disenchantment (Section 3), irritation (Section 4), and detachment (Section 5). In Section 6, I will address the consequences of this circuit for the political bond. Finally, in Section 7, I will present some concluding reflections regarding the analytical scope of the circuit of detachment. A disclaimer before continuing: Some of the ideas presented here have already been discussed in various published texts, especially in Spanish.[6] Inevitably, then, although the context is new, I will be restating some previously published ideas and arguments. It is worth bearing in mind that long-haul intellectual work necessarily involves reflecting on one's own ideas to refine or transform them along the way (Tilly 2005). The production and advancement of knowledge are rarely linear, even if only because we often must retrace our steps to recover an idea that we had left behind.

---

[5] A research journey is always a collective enterprise. I am profoundly indebted to each of the members of the research teams which took part in the different empirical works carried out in the last almost two decades. But I am specially indebted to Danilo Martuccelli for his theoretical inspiration and his intellectual generosity.

[6] Consequently, priority will be given to references to the publications in which the specific results were presented and the arguments deriving from them were defended. In the case of direct quotations, the reader will be referred to the research study from which the quotation is taken.

2 Excessiveness

2.1 Neoliberalism and the Historical Condition

2.1.1 Neoliberalism As a Concept and Model

Neoliberalism is the name given to a type of economic model based on the imperative of promoting free markets and on the belief that market self-regulation via competition will benefit the economy. With variations, the model depends on the deregulation of individuals' relationships with the market and envisions the state's role as limited to safeguarding competitive practices in the market. As a correlate, the neoliberal model envisions the state abandoning many areas of social provision previously within its purview. Neoliberalism promotes depoliticization by prioritizing an economic and moral vision of society; legitimizes a perspective centered on the individual, rather than on collective structures; and aspires to understand and mold society on the basis of these principles, institutions, and relational modes (Amable 2011; Davies 2014). Finally, neoliberalism's most visible political and economic effects in recent decades have been the growing importance of the financial sector, a sharp increase in inequality, a significant increase in returns to capital at the cost of diminished returns to labor, and altered ways of thinking about collective experience (Harvey 2005; Streeck 2011).

Neoliberalism takes various forms depending on the country in which it occurs. Chile was one of the first countries in the world to change its policies and institutions based on neoliberal principles. Chile began with a series of economic measures that progressively took shape as a "model," including privatization of state companies; the state's retreat from the direct provision of social services, and the subsequent commercialization of these services; a state based upon the principle of subsidiarity; economic liberalization and deregulation; the opening of markets to international competition; and labor flexibility, among others (Salazar and Pinto 1999; Ruiz and Boccardo 2015). These measures aligned with neoliberal principles: they eroded a redistributive conception of social protection, weakened worker protections and forms of collective labor organization, strengthened individual solutions over collective ones, and promoted an economistic view of society.

Chile's implementation of neoliberal policies, introduced after the 1973 coup under the military regime of General Augusto Pinochet (1973–90) by the so-called Chilean Chicago Boys, who were taught and directly influenced by Milton Friedman (Valdés 1995), encountered some obstacles over time and underwent various modifications along the way (Büchi 2008). First, in the 1980s, power shifted to a more pragmatic team that gave greater scope for state action and proposed new measures in response to the country's serious economic crisis (Collier and Sater 1999). Second, adjustments occurred that made the business sector a major social actor (Ruiz and Boccardo 2015). Third, consolidation of the model occurred in association with the return to democracy in 1990 and the subsequent twenty years of uninterrupted government by the Coalition of Parties for Democracy.[7]

A distinctive aspect of Chilean neoliberalism is the oligopolistic control of markets with an extreme concentration of property in most sectors of the economy (Ruiz and Boccardo 2015), a phenomenon Schneider (2013) has called *hierarchical capitalism*. Another distinguishing feature is that the model's consolidation benefited from a surge of wealth in the Latin American region due to the so-called commodity boom that began in the mid-2000s. This boom was particularly spectacular in a country whose economy depends more on income from natural resources – primarily from copper mining – than does the economy of any other Latin American country (Ordóñez and Silva 2019).

The conception of the functions of the state was a very important aspect of the neoliberal model. Within the neoliberal framework, the state's role was to be reduced to supplying what other actors, such as families, private parties, or individuals, could not or would not supply. State economic intervention was to occur only in extreme cases, and the state was not the only entity that could provide social services; private companies also could serve as providers.

Chile's adoption of the neoliberal model resulted in a sharp reduction in state provision of social services and protections. The erosion of the ideal of universal provision of services and protections to the entire population in favor of support targeted at very vulnerable groups (Raczynski 1994) undermined the feelings of solidarity that form the core of the social bond. One effect of this erosion was that Chileans lacked adequate protection from predatory market actors, leaving them vulnerable to the "fine print," or abuses.

2.1.2 Neoliberalism Experienced

At the same time, "neoliberalism" is the name Chileans give to what they call the "system" or "model" shaping their day-to-day lives. Chileans recognize this "system" as one of the two factors that give form to the combination of constraints and challenges that must be faced in social life, that is, as one of the factors that shape their historical condition (the second factor, discussed in Section 3.2, is the pressure to democratize social relations) (Araujo and Martuccelli 2012).

---

[7] The so-called coalition did not alter either the productive or the economic structure in any essential aspect, but it developed an increasingly successful network of social protection for the most vulnerable (Espinoza, Barozet, and Méndez 2013; Garretón 2012).

The term figures increasingly in individuals' accounts of their lives from the early 2000s until the present day.

Unlike the way neoliberalism is typically discussed in European and North American debates on the subject, in Chile the term refers to a system that seems to many Chileans to have been imposed on them by force rather than because of any belief they may have had in it. Indeed, since the late 1990s, the consequences of neoliberalism have been viewed increasingly critically across society, except perhaps by the most privileged and protected members of society. Yet, these criticisms tell only one side of the story, for Chileans can point to various ways in which neoliberalism has benefited the country.

For example, Chile has experienced a reduction in poverty. While the exact numbers remain subject to debate,[8] there is no question that the prevalence of poverty has decreased, or at least that its nature has changed. A new face of poverty has emerged, linked to increased access to consumer goods. The increased availability of household appliances and other household goods lies at the heart of this change. In 1987, 7 percent of households with the lowest income owned three assets such as a washing machine, a television, a refrigerator, or a gas cooker. By 2002, about 74 percent of households in this income bracket owned three or more of these items (Ariztía 2004). Beyond a simple question of status, this increase in ownership of durable goods brought about a real improvement in Chileans' quality of life. Between 1992 and 2002, a third of the needy Chilean households obtained electricity for the first time. During the same period, the percentage of poor urban households that lacked access to potable water dropped from 20 percent to 8 percent (Ramos 2004).

Another especially important change has been the increase in levels of schooling and the new groups that have received higher education. In 1992, 46.49 percent of Chileans over 25 years old reported that primary school was their highest level of education and only 11.7 percent reported having completed postsecondary studies (e.g., in universities, technology institutes, technical education centers). By 2017, the percentage of the adult population who had completed only primary school had dropped to 25.6 percent while the percentage of those who completed higher education had risen to 29.8 percent (INE 2017).

---

[8] There have been changes in the measurement of poverty. In 2009, it changed from a one-dimensional, income-based measurement to a multifactorial measurement comprising four dimensions until 2015, and thereafter comprising five dimensions. Despite the variation in the percentages produced by each type of measurement – the percentage of the population living in poverty in 2017 measured by income was 8.6 percent; with four factors, it was 18.6 percent; and with five factors, 20.7 percent – all of them show a downward trend (MINDES 2020).

These changes in the level of educational attainment involve achievements and experiences that represent true watersheds in family histories. In 2014, 49 percent of Chileans felt their social status had improved compared with that of their parents. The majority also reported that their level of income (58 percent), work situation (54 percent), and family life (53 percent) had improved, a perception that has only increased since. For example, in 2019, 62 percent of people surveyed considered that their income was better or much better than that of their parents (PUC 2019).

A great many of my interviewees from the working- and middle-class sectors (Inv. 2 and 5) have memories of the much harsher living conditions of their grandparents or even parents. Earthen floors, a lack of shoes, and even hunger stand out in the stories they narrate of their childhoods. As the youngest interviewees acknowledge, the opportunities they have had are different and far better than those available to their parents or grandparents. Family historical memory, then, yields a positive evaluation of how far the country has progressed combined with the hope that their children will do still better. Additionally, this feeling of improvement is associated with a sense of greater proximity to other social groups, which has contributed to raised expectations and a change in beliefs about what one can legitimately aspire to achieve.

This optimistic assessment, however, coexists with another certainty: that the costs of these quality of life improvements are disproportionately borne on the shoulders of ordinary folk. That is, collective betterment has come hand-in-hand with a transfer to individuals of the management of their own social integration. This transfer has manifested in individuals having to face an accumulation of excessive demands in their everyday lives. These experiences at first were associated with a diffuse malaise, as diagnosed by the Programa de Naciones Unidas para el Desarrollo (PNUD) in the late 1990s, but came to nurture various feelings of discontent, increasingly accompanied by strong doses of anger and indignation.

2.2 The Faces of Excessiveness

I use the word *excessiveness* to refer to the quality of structural demands or exigencies individuals must confront in their ordinary social lives: immoderate demands that involve an incessant drive to action, which create the perception of being overtaxed and under pressure, and that very often are experienced as a breach of one's limits (physical, health, motivational, psychic, etc.). Many types of excessiveness can be identified (Inv. 2; Araujo and Martuccelli 2012). Examples include excessive experience of vulnerability (living without a safety net); the excessive demands of the ideal fostered by neoliberalism (competition, self-effort, performance, and materialism, among others); excessive pressure to adapt to historical changes by developing new skills and inventing new strategies; and excessive inequality (in the distribution of goods and wealth). For reasons of space, I will not describe these in detail but will concentrate on two other examples of excessiveness that seem especially threatening for people in their everyday lives: excessiveness in work and in the management of time.

2.2.1 Excessiveness in Work

Once installed, the new model confronted individuals with the need to deal with new circumstances as economic and labor subjects. The workplace under the impact of the 1979 Labor Plan promulgated by the Pinochet military dictatorship has been characterized by the normalization of precarious and flexible terms of employment, as well as weakened worker protections and collective bargaining power (Ramos 2009; PNUD 2017; Julián 2018). The new framework of labor relations is based on individualization, commodification, and decollectivization (Stecher and Sisto 2019). Added to this are the low wage levels of much of the population. By 2020, two out of three workers were earning less than CLP 550,000 after tax (the equivalent of USD 750 per month in 2020 and USD 600 currently) (Durán and Kremerman 2020). The changes also brought a notable intensification of work and new subject ideals (Soto and Fardella 2019).

From the perspective of individuals, the installation of the neoliberal model and its consequences shape what could be considered the central feature experienced in the world of work: its excessiveness. This can be seen in everyday life from the various ways in which individuals have had to deal with the challenges of work. As an example, let us analyze just one of them: *pluriactivity.*

There are two types of pluriactivity: serial pluriactivity, that is, careers during which the type of employment varies substantially, and simultaneous pluriactivity, in which people perform different jobs during the same period for different employers (for example, adding a weekend job), engage in diverse independent activities (for example, working in multiple small enterprises), or a combination of both. Unlike in other countries, such as in Europe, where a single work activity tends to be the norm (Mouriaux 2006), pluriactivity is a common practice among people in Chile today, especially but not exclusively among those in the popular sectors (Araujo and Martuccelli 2012: Vol. II, 18–31).[9]

---

[9] I use "popular sectors" to refer to lower-income sections of the population that share not only economic traits but also social and cultural ones.

A compelling reason for the expansion of pluriactivity is that it functions, like credit and indebtedness, as a backstop that allows a standard of living to be maintained when wages from a single job are insufficient to cover living costs. Such costs have been strongly impacted by the reduction in good quality state-sponsored social provision (particularly in the areas of health and education), by changes in expectations and definitions of a decent minimum income, and by insufficient state regulation of the market that determines the costs of services and goods.[10] Added to these increased costs is the constant feeling of insecurity arising from the lack of labor protections.

Indeed, with the reduced wages they receive, many families have had to deal with the rapid privatization of education and health services and the erosion of their quality. In 1987, an average family spent 3.76 percent of its income on education, while in 2017 it spent 5.6 percent on this item (INE 1988; INE 2017). Of the OECD countries, families in Chile pay the highest percentage (34 percent) of education costs, compared with an OECD average of 12 percent (OECD 2020). The increase is important not only for the middle-income sectors but also for lower-income sectors. Owing to parents' evaluation of municipal (free) schools as extremely poor, recent decades saw a significant student migration to subsidized private schools (schools receiving state support but to which parents contribute a monthly fee).[11] From 2006 to 2020, enrollment in municipal schools decreased by 33.4 percent, while it increased in subsidized private establishments by 14.3 percent and in fee-paying schools by 22.8 percent (MINEDUC 2020). By 2020 subsidized private schools constituted 54.4 percent of the students enrolled in the school system, fee-paying private institutions 9 percent, and municipal schools only 32.5 percent (MINEDUC 2021).

The same is true of health provision. The Chilean health system comprises three different forms of administration. One is exclusively for the armed forces and law enforcement personnel, and the other two are accessible to the civil population: the state-run National Health Fund (FONASA) and the private healthcare insurance companies (ISAPRE), the latter created under Augusto

---

[10] Alfredo, a worker from the popular sectors, is a good example. He works "from 6:00 in the morning until midnight" so with the money he earns from overtime, he can buy "a cooker with two gas canisters and also a dining table" (Inv. 2).

[11] The Chilean school education system consists of five different forms of management: municipal schools (public schools administered by local governments at the municipal level); local public education services (since 2018; they are meant to replace municipal administration); delegated administration corporations (corporations that manage state educational establishments); private subsidized schools (partial public subsidies for private schooling); and private schools. According to the Ministry of Education (MINEDUC 2020), during 2020, 54.35 percent of students were enrolled in private subsidized schools, 32.46 percent in municipal schools, 9.01 percent in private schools, 2.95 percent in local public education services, and 1.23 percent in delegated administration corporations

Pinochet's regime. Salaried workers must contribute 7 percent of their wages to FONASA, but since Pinochet's reforms workers have been allowed to use this mandatory expenditure to purchase private health insurance. Gradually, due to the increased cost of private health insurance, individuals have been required to pay extra fees to remain in the private healthcare system. Many, therefore, have had to return to the public system. According to FONASA (2018), in 2018 there were 18,929,311 people assigned to the health system. Of these, 75.2 percent belonged to FONASA, 18 percent to ISAPRE, and 6.8 percent to the health system of the armed forces and law enforcement personnel. Beneficiaries of FONASA are grouped into four tranches according to their monthly taxable income: A – people without economic resources (including migrants) and people who receive family subsidy; B – people earning income equal to or less than the established minimum wage (MW), around $390; C – people earning more than MW but less than $576; and D – people earning over $576. The first two groups receive a bonus of 100 percent for healthcare provision. For group C, the bonus covers 90 percent and for group D, only 80 percent of healthcare expenses.[12] As a result, according to the OECD (2019), the average percentage of healthcare expenditure that Chileans pay out-of-pocket (33.5 percent) is the fifth highest of all the OECD member countries. Out-of-pocket expenses are the direct payments people make when using health benefits. According to INE (2017), healthcare costs account for 7.6 percent on average of Chileans' monthly household expenditures.

Moreover, this high expense rate is accompanied by dissatisfaction with the healthcare system, especially the public one. Research has shown that the long waits for care, the deficiencies of the healthcare system, the poor treatment received, and the awareness that money plays a prominent role in securing rights and respectful treatment led Chileans to expect better service in the private sector (similar considerations led them to also expect better education in the private sector) (Araujo 2009: 70–77). For example, during the so-called social outbreak of 2019, one of the most important forms of expression was the ubiquitous graffiti and protesters' banners and placards. These not only served to express demands but often posed counterarguments to the authorities and commented on their decisions. The following was one of the many expressions

---

[12] Two types of care established by the health benefits system are available through FONASA. One type is the Institutional Care Modality (MAI). It is available to all groups and medical benefits are granted by the agencies that make up the National System of Health Services, which are dependent on the Ministry of Health, or by public or private entities with which the health services or FONASA have reached agreements for this purpose. The second type is a voucher system, the Modality of Free Choice (MLE), available for groups B, C, and D. Here the beneficiaries freely choose the professional and/or entity under the tuition and control of FONASA, from the public or private sector, registered in the role of FONASA.

that challenged authorities' statements about the violence of the protesters: "VIOLENCE is the fact that my patients ask, 'and do you know how much it would cost if I do it privately?' BECAUSE THEY ARE TERRIFIED OF HAVING TO CONTINUE WAITING" (Molina 2020: 38). In fact, by 2018 the number of patients who were waiting for a consultation in a new specialty (non-GES)[13] was 1.5 million and their average waiting time was 483 days. The COVID-19 pandemic increased the number of people on this waiting list. By mid-2020 there were already 1.7 million (Bastias et al. 2020).

Apart from the increased cost of living, the pressure for pluriactivity was also accentuated by the widening gap between needs and expectations and the reduced purchasing power of wages. The definition of minimally decent (and necessary) living standards changed radically over this period. A pertinent example is spending on communications, now considered a basic good and a factor in social integration. The percentage of household expenditure on communication increased from 0.97 percent of the family budget to 5.3 percent between 1978 and 2017. A major reason for this was the increase in the number of items in this category. In 1978, the category basically consisted of telephone bills, while in 2017 it consisted of thirty-three items, including mobile phones and internet connections (INE 2017).

Another factor encouraging pluriactivity is status insecurity (positional inconsistency), a phenomenon that affects how an individual's social position is structured (Araujo and Martuccelli 2012: Vol. I, 125–159). Aside from those who compose a small, durable, and globally protected group (in a country that has an extreme concentration of wealth and power),[14] most individuals feel that their social position is extremely susceptible to deterioration. Although, of course, such vulnerability varies by social sector, various potentially destabilizing events can happen to people in all sectors without warning and drastically affect both their career and their social position. A serious illness or acquired disability is the most feared eventuality. It may produce a sharp drop in status since the only way to cope with it, aside from intrafamily solidarity – or, in the case of popular sectors, raising funds from neighbors by holding events such as bingo games or raffles[15] – is by accruing debt that is impossible to repay.

---

[13] The Explicit Health Guarantees (GES) apply only to a limited and specific list of diseases. Special benefits are guaranteed by law to people affected by these diseases whether they are affiliated with FONASA or ISAPRE. The waiting lists for consultation of new specialties correspond to the pathologies not included in the list covered by the GES.

[14] According to the World Inequality Database (WID 2019), in 2019, 10 percent of the population of Chile earned 60.2 percent of all income, while 1 percent earned 27.8 percent of all income and the bottom 50 percent of the population earned only 10.1 percent of the total income.

[15] Another example seen on a Santiago wall during the 2019 protests: "No + Raffles or Bingos. X a decent health" (Molina 2020: 66).

Whatever the reason, pluriactivity essentially helps heighten the sensation of excessiveness. It is associated with high levels of stress and is often linked to jobs that either afford little protection or are purely informal, increasing vulnerability. It both produces high levels of individual burnout and erodes workers' perceived physical and mental health.[16]

2.2.2 Excessiveness in the Management of Time

The growing prevalence of pluriactivity, coupled with the general trends in the nature of work experience, has direct consequences for how much time work consumes. One of the most common experiences in Chile today is a feeling of saturation and fatigue produced by the perception of "endless work" that eats into family and personal time. For pluriactive wage earners, as one of my interviewees said, it means having to make "the schedules fit"; for independent workers or owners of small- and medium-sized businesses, the overinvestment of time is constant and structural due to the fragility they perceive in their activities. In the various studies I conducted, interviewees frequently mentioned working ten-hour or twelve-hour days.[17] Long working days, however, are common even among wage earners with somewhat less precarious jobs. In these cases, the overinvestment of time is due to working overtime or to the "logic of presence" – a widespread expectation in the world of work that the worker should remain in the workplace for as long as possible, without there necessarily being a reasonable justification for it or any productivity consequences. "Keeping the chair warm," as several interviewees pointed out, is taken as an indicator of being a good worker. For many interviewees, this logic was counterproductive; it made them less productive and served simply as an informal control mechanism, but its effects were powerful since it was experienced as a veiled threat (Araujo and Martuccelli 2012: Vol. II, 161–172). To all of the above must be added the demands of commuting times, a special problem for residents of Santiago, the country's capital, and a particular hardship for the popular sectors. Santiago residents can spend up to two hours commuting each morning (CNDU 2020).

---

[16] Work leave for mental illness represents the second-largest expense in medical leave applications granted: 53.8 percent for depressive episodes, 21.8 percent for anxiety disorders, and 16.8 percent for severe stress and adjustment disorders. Note also that the segment of the population with the highest prevalence of depressive symptoms is those of working age (Errázuriz et al. 2015).

[17] Adolfo, a young professional in his early thirties, states, "I work a lot. I am in a crisis, in fact, because I am very tired in fact, because I work a lot. I work every day, Saturdays included ... So they are long working days, 12, 14 hours" (Inv. 2). This quotation is representative of many of the testimonies recorded in this and other investigations.

The time-greedy nature of work has important consequences for the experience of imbalance in time management, which is widespread throughout society. The feeling of suffocation that many report is associated with time being confiscated by work, with much less of it available for associative activities or for free time.[18] Most problematic for people, however, is the squeezing of time left available for the family sphere. This arouses intense feelings of tension, conflict, and guilt, especially for women. In the case of men, the persistence of their role as economic provider works as a protective shield against these feelings.

Normatively speaking, the family is the most important sphere. By "family," we refer to the couple and/or their children – the inner, closest circle – but also to their outer circle: parents or other significant relatives. The normative preeminence of family obligations is not only linked to the historical weight of kinship relations and the family in Chile and the Latin American region as a whole but also to the contemporary fact that family is the most significant source of support needed to face social life. According to my findings, when an individual must respond to structural demands on their own, the family is the resource most often mobilized to solve problems of housing, health, and the most common childcare issues, or to provide small "rescue" loans at moments of temporary economic difficulty.

Family relationships, however, need to be cared for and cultivated purposefully and carefully. Time is a resource of the utmost importance for this cultivation. This is due to the predominance of "clan-like" forms of relationship and a strongly legitimized family sociability. The clannish character is expressed in the well-defined boundaries and a certain closedness with which family sociability tends to be structured, with strong commitments and ritual demands as well as rigidly defined roles (Araujo and Martuccelli 2012: Vol. II, 168–181).

Caught between these conflicting needs – the nonnegotiable demands of the world of work, the feeling of falling short in one's family obligations, nostalgia for associative activities, and the need for personal time – the effort to manage one's time is an overwhelming experience. It is yet another expression of the multiple excesses that pervade contemporary social experience.

---

[18] Verónica is a woman from the popular sectors who works making clothing. She says that she has no time for social life: "Every day I have the problem of needing to make money, producing clothing items, then I fall asleep at 1:00 or 2:00 in the morning and start working at 6:00 in the morning."

2.3 Excessiveness and Individuals

Social change, for normative and material structural reasons that lie at the heart of the Chilean historical condition, has forced individuals to develop new skills, performances, and self-representations to face a life shaped by constant uncertainty and material and moral instability. Moreover, it is a transformation that, as a study in progress shows, occurs in a context in which individualism, in its combined juridical, economic, and social expressions, appears for the first time in the history of the country as a true and legitimized social ideal (Inv. 8).

At the same time, this need for hyperactivity takes the form of an enormous effort to mobilize informal supports. Individuals are driven to become *relational hyper-actors* (Araujo and Martuccelli 2014). Outcomes have shown that, as a result of their experiences, individuals develop a new and fortified self-image and increased confidence in their own capacities. Experiences, now dating back several decades, of facing social life individually, or with only the help they are able to get from their close kin and associates, have led individuals to view themselves as capable of coping with social life on their own. In this sense, these findings do not support the claim (PNUD 2015) that Chileans' strengthened self-image is primarily attributable to political factors. Paradoxically, it is the demands this new economic and social model places on Chileans in their everyday life that has inadvertently led Chileans to view themselves as more capable people.

However, this stronger self-image has had unexpected consequences. For example, Chileans increasingly believe that it is possible and even desirable to act without institutions, a belief related to the feeling of detachment. To appreciate this phenomenon in all its nuance, we must first look closely at the second component of the circuit: disenchantment.

3 Disenchantment

3.1 The Neoliberal Promise

The neoliberal model promised Chileans a better life. From the beginning, the model's implementation was accompanied by the idea that social and economic improvements depended on individual effort. This idea permeated all forms of social organization by impacting labor relations; relations between the state and its citizens; the role of the market; and people's own practices and beliefs. This early association between the improvement of people's living conditions and individual effort is present in one of the slogans of the Pinochet dictatorship: "Make proletarians into owners" (Pinedo 1997: 5).

The individualization of responsibility for one's own social existence ended up producing new strategies for coping with social life and, as we saw, had the unintended effect of strengthening individuals' estimation of their abilities and capacity to cope with social life on their own. At the same time, however, such enhanced capacity was linked to growing disappointment with the unfulfilled promises of the model and individuals' perception that the costs were being disproportionately borne on their shoulders.

The role of economic inequality as a factor contributing to this disenchantment has been much debated. According to the PNUD (2017), whereas in 2000 only 42 percent of survey respondents strongly agreed that income differences in the country were very large, by 2017 90 percent of respondents espoused this view. However, this sensitivity to structural economic inequalities developed slowly and disenchantment had three major sources: the existence of a ceiling on people's possibilities for improvement; frustration at the low returns to personal effort; and the experience that, even after certain improvements were achieved, people often suffered a deterioration in their situation.

3.1.1 Ceilings and Borders

Expectations of social mobility are perhaps one of the clearest expressions of how people perceive the existence of a ceiling blocking improvements to their quality of life. Neoliberalism made two promises: One was that effort would allow people to ascend the social ladder. The other was that the popular sectors or working classes would enter the ranks of the middle classes in increasing numbers. Both promises failed to materialize. Using data from 2009, Espinoza, Barozet, and Méndez (2013) argued that even then the social structure was becoming more rigid: Chileans were less likely to be in a substantially different occupational class from that of their parents than ten years previously. The expectation that many people from the less advantaged socioeconomic groups would enter the middle class proved illusory (pp. 182, 187). Furthermore, as Pérez-Ahumada (2018) has pointed out in a study of changes to the Chilean class structure between 1992 and 2013, the growth of the middle class has been relatively marginal. Rather, the trend has gone in the other direction: it was the working class that grew between 2003 and 2013. In the last year of the study, the informally self-employed and the working class together accounted for around 75 percent of the population (182).

Of course, what can be deduced from these structural data is not necessarily reflected directly or immediately in people's perceptions of their social status. Nevertheless, qualitative data do show a steady waning of belief in these promises of upward mobility. To take one example, until the 2010s, my studies showed that popular sector Chileans espoused a class-based explanation for their social experiences – that is, things happened to them because they were poor – but in their global perceptions of society, "the poor" always referred to others, not to themselves (Inv. 1 and 2; Araujo 2009). This partly explains why so many consider themselves to be middle class. At present, the attribution of typical experiences to their social position, the importance of their position in structuring their demands, and their positional identity are all closer to one another, as can be seen from an analysis of recent material (Inv. 6). The poor are also themselves.

3.1.2 Poor Rewards

The second ingredient of disenchantment, the perception of poor returns to individual effort, begins with an aspect that we have already discussed: low wages, or low income in the case of those who work independently. This perception is found across the different socioeconomic sectors. It is present, for example, in the sentiments of Eduardo, a designer in his thirties from the popular sectors, who explains that he has only just enough to scrape by: "I pay my rent, I pay my water, electricity and *chao* [that's it], there are times when I don't even have enough left to eat." But it is also true of Fabiola, an event planner from the wealthy middle sectors who became seriously ill due to overwork; her strenuous effort served only "to pay the bills" (Inv. 2).

But low wages are not the only aspect of disenchantment with the poor returns to effort invested. Education is another. The expansion of access to higher education has been an especially notable phenomenon in recent decades. The number of students who are the first in their families to attend college is considerable. This expansion, which promised integration and upward mobility, has entailed dedicated effort by families, but also by young people themselves taking out loans to pay for it. More than a third of higher education students finance their studies out of family resources, but about a quarter contract loans, while 16.6 percent work while they study. Only 17 percent have a scholarship and 5 percent pay for their studies with their savings (Cox, Hernando, and Rebolledo 2018: 40). Student loans have been a particular source of debate and of student movements' demands since 2011. They generate high levels of long-term debt so that, as some have argued, in order to study, young people end up mortgaging their future and lowering their aspirations.

Moreover, efforts invested in higher education have generally not yielded the expected payoffs. First, because educational qualifications lost value as they became commonplace, the type of qualification needed to secure better opportunities in the job market was constantly upgraded. Thus, although educational qualifications still affect job opportunities because the overall rate of return remains positive in the country, they are by no means a guarantee of social mobility to match people's expectations. The precariousness of the labor market is a factor in this, but the distribution of opportunities is also highly dependent on factors such as social background, appearance, and surname (PNUD 2017). However, while it is true that opportunities are not obtained solely with a degree, and opportunities are often dependent on a network of contacts or strongly influenced by class, education paradoxically continues to be seen as the only element that could eventually be relied on to counterbalance the power of these personal networks (Araujo and Martuccelli 2012). This may explain why, despite their onerous experience of taking out loans to pursue higher education, 63 percent of young people between 18 and 29 years old consider the financial burden worthwhile; they do not consider it an (undue) debt, but an investment (INJUV 2020).

3.1.3 Deterioration

A third stream contributing to disenchantment is the experience of one's situation deteriorating rather than improving. The case of housing is a good example. According to Rasse (2019), in the 1980s and 1990s, the popular sectors' access to housing increased, and this meant a drastic reduction of the housing shortage. However, the trend subsequently reversed. According to Rasse, this was an outcome of the substandard quality of the newly constructed homes and weak efforts at urban social integration, due to the location of these homes on the city's periphery where there existed few opportunities for work, health, education, and recreation. Despite the government's social policies and the various programs implemented to improve neighborhood infrastructure and resident satisfaction, a large percentage of the social housing stock progressively deteriorated.

Indeed, much of the feeling of positional inconsistency detected in my studies was related to the deterioration of interviewees' neighborhoods, due to both the poor quality of services and, especially, the growing threat of drugs and crime. For many, this deterioration not only threatened the quality of everyday life and their children's future but very specifically the value of their homes, which they had acquired with great effort. For many, their home was the most important asset they had to provide some permanence to their social status (Araujo and Martuccelli 2012: Vol. I, 148–154; Inv. 2 and 5).

At the same time, the deterioration of living standards is manifested in the ever-greater difficulty experienced by new low-income households in gaining access to housing, due to an increase in land prices resulting from the lack of regulation and the speculative strategies of real estate investors. This has led to a higher number of people living in *campamentos* (self-built informal settlements) and of *allegados* (families forced to lodge with close relatives). In the Metropolitan Region of Santiago, the number of *allegados* increased from 37,319 to 175,377 between 2000 and 2017 (Rasse 2019: 111).

A second example is indebtedness and overindebtedness. According to the Central Bank (2020), for the second half of 2020, the total debt of households equaled 76.4 percent of their disposable income, the highest level of indebtedness in the country's history. While debt initially promised access to goods and lifestyle improvements, it became for many in Chile an oppressive way of life, a destabilizing routine. As Marta, a paramedic from the popular sectors, put it, most Chileans "live our whole lives in debt ... You ask the bank for some money, you pay it, you finish paying it ... and back you go into debt!" (Inv. 2). But this experience is not limited to the popular sectors. Mariana, a middle-class woman, commented: "The debts are what have most people feeling so overwhelmed, the debts trap you and take your life away. I had a really bad time, really bad, I even got to the point of wanting to take pills [to commit suicide: KA] out of desperation" (Inv. 5).

The neoliberal model involved the financialization of the economy and even of many aspects of social life (Harvey 2005: 33). In Chile, as in other Latin American countries, the expansion of consumer culture went hand in hand with access to credit. Between 1997 and 2005, the number of credit cards for every 100,000 inhabitants increased from 1,520 to 2,365. Similarly, credit card use during this period increased by 139 percent (Morales and Yáñez 2006). Access to credit for low-income individuals was also facilitated by credit offerings from non-banking institutions (i.e., retailers).

Many critics of the neoliberal model make a direct link between debt and the culture of consumerism, which they considered a central factor in cultivating feelings of alienation among the population (Moulian 1998). My studies showed, however, consistent with other findings, that consumerism should not be considered merely a hedonistic expression of alienation. Consumption is often a tool that helps make care transactions possible in a family or neighborhood (Han 2012). Credit and debt, moreover, have served to close the gap created by the combination of low wages, the rise in the cost of living, and new beliefs about what constitutes a minimally decent living standard. Credit also eases the intense pressure for the preservation of status among the more affluent sectors (Araujo and Martuccelli 2012: Vol. I, 65–71).

Overindebtedness is a problem that has long existed in the United States and European countries, but it has tended to be interpreted as a conflict between modern, consumerist values on the one hand and those of simplicity or moderation on the other (Bell 1976; Beck 1992). By contrast, in Chile over-indebtedness is strongly associated with a society that has collectively shaken off responsibility for the personal fate of its members. This abnegation of responsibility can be seen in the preservation of structural traits that force people to rely on credit and indebtedness to meet basic needs. It can be seen in the weak regulation of interest rates, particularly the rates of the retailer-issued credit cards most commonly used by the popular sectors. It can be seen in the absence of efforts to build collective awareness of reasonable credit limits, instead of devolving to individuals the responsibility for defining moral or pragmatic boundaries to protect themselves against excessive debt (Inv. 2 and 5).

But disenchantment is not only a matter of the promises derived from the economic model. It is also strongly linked – and this has been its most important early expression – with disappointment over the promises associated with the pressure for democratization of social relations.

3.2 The Promise of Democratization

3.2.1 Equality and Subjects of Law

In Chile, both the collapse of democracy in the early 1970s and its return in the 1990s were active moments in the configuration and reaffirmation of democratic values. During the dictatorship, "democracy" was a hope and an objective while with the end of the dictatorship, in the early 1990s, it became a task. The task was achieved only to a limited extent. Despite this fact – and this point is central – the discourse of citizenship, the notion of rights, and the principle of equality were strongly asserted. While this discourse was not new to Chile or the region, it underwent a new expansive wave as the democratization processes unfolded (Dagnino, Olivera, and Panfichi 2006, among others), forming part of the so-called process of *citizenization* in Latin America (Domingues 2009).

The model of the individual as a holder of rights and the ideal of equality that underlies it were increasingly championed as normative ideals by different actors. Thus, the task of strengthening law as a legitimate and efficient regulatory ideal of society permeated the task of modernizing the state, making law a basis for the declaration of principles regarding the conception of society, its individuals, and its relations with them (Drake and Jaksic 2002). The model was promoted by the institutional political system and gradually also by conservative sectors, most forcefully in their version of equal opportunity. Social movements – especially, but not only, feminist groups – also participated in promoting the ideal of equality and, in line with the international trend, shifted their demands toward the paradigm of rights and citizenship (Garretón 2000).

They broadened the fields in which equality was to be applied, extending it from the purely socioeconomic field to include others such as the struggles of women, Indigenous peoples, or sexual minorities (Vargas 2008). These developments took place in the context of a heightened receptivity to the agendas of international organizations, the United Nations system, and other institutions such as the Inter-American Development Bank and the World Bank.

The spread of the promise of equality, of course, has also had very important cultural inputs. The media have played a very signifcant role in this context, by transmitting relational models that reflect and encourage greater equality. For example, national soap operas began to show active, self-sufficient, and capable women who gained space in dramatic conflicts; children began to be represented on television as agents and not only as objects of adult decisions (Vergara, Chávez, and Vergara 2010). Moreover, access to the Internet was growing, which allowed greater access to other content and debates, as well as more horizontal forms of participation. Finally, mention should be made of sociodemographic changes, particularly the significant increase in access to education.

Of course, an intention to spread new principles or representations does not necessarily mean that they are adopted in practice. In a study carried out in the mid-2000s (Inv. 1), I set out to discover the fate of these normative possibilities. My findings showed that people recognized rights as being ideal attributes that were available to subjects to build an idea of themselves, but what they mainly took from the concept was the promise that it conveyed: equality (Inv. 1; Araujo 2009). Equality was no longer the domain of enlightened "vanguards"; it had become an ever-present reference point used by ordinary individuals to judge and evaluate their daily experiences in society.

A key finding of this study, confirmed in others that followed, was that people's preferred understanding of the term "equality" concerned the treatment of individuals in everyday interactions. This translated into new expectations of horizontality in such relationships. *Expectations of horizontality* refers to the hope that an interaction involving the management of asymmetries will be based on recognition of a basic equality between the participants; that they will receive the same treatment in everyday interactions regardless of their social status, the symbols of distinction that the other can mobilize, or the relationship to power that they can display. It is a demand directed both to institutions and to others that helps restore the signs of personal dignity and the preferred indicators of respect (Araujo 2013).

But while individuals recognized and adopted these ideals and expectations, their everyday experiences showed them a different reality. Four systemic social logics persisted, which continued to structure interactions. These logics belied the power of the ideal normative principles. Individuals recognized them as historically prevalent logics in Chilean society (Araujo 2013).

First is the logic of naturalized hierarchies. This presumes the importance of ascribed traits (family origin, skin color, etc.) in a highly vertical relational architecture, expressed, for example, in the widespread feeling of the popular sectors that the only eyes that see them are the eyes of surveillants (Araujo 2009: 45–58).

Second is the logic of privilege, based on gender and generational and ethnic criteria, but mainly on class. It is a logic embodied, for example, in fake meritocracy, in nepotism – a recurring practice of the political class – or in a society in which surname and family networks are crucial in determining opportunities.

Third is the logic of authoritarianism, perceived as a manner of exercising authority that is pervasive and extends throughout society; a manner that makes force, whether virtual or real, into a permanent possibility and demands machine-like obedience from those over whom it is exercised (Araujo 2016).

Fourth is the logic of the exercise of power, where the unregulated use of power and confrontation defines access to goods, prerogatives over their use, or a person's very place in society. Thanks to the action of this logic, the social space is perceived as a space for the exercise of power. As a participant in one of my studies said: in this society, "the strongest puts his foot on the weakest"; no matter what type of relationship it is, there is one who can "always put his foot on someone else" (Inv. 1).

The clash between expectations of horizontality and the continuing reality of these logics has undermined the promise of equality, with very important consequences. It has brought about the emergence of a new sensibility, a new appraisal and judgment of the customary practices of actors, whether of the upper classes, politicians, or of other individuals encountered in everyday interactions. This has been expressed in the importance now given to what we have called *interactional inequalities*, a particular type of inequality centered on patterns of face-to-face inter-action whose main content is mistreatment or abuse.[19] It has spotlighted the contradictions of a society that likes to appear modern and egalitarian and has even proposed institutional mechanisms designed to achieve this state, but is actually organized by a deeply vertical social bond. The term "abuse," often used by my interviewees in the 2000s, became an expression

---

[19] A type of inequality whose lack of legitimacy has grown over time. According to measurements carried out in recent years, interactional inequalities are the ones most resented by people in Chile (in all socioeconomic sectors and age ranges studied); they are resented much more than economic inequalities (PNUD 2015: 99).

commonly used to refer to that which they found intolerable. By the latter part of the 2010s, "abuse" had found its way into public discussion, had become politicized, and was one of the most important terms for referring to the unacceptable, the morally unjustifiable, and the politically unpardonable (Inv. 7).

However, the force of social experience led, paradoxically, to the fact that, although people criticized the social logics described above and demanded that they change, individuals did not necessarily alter how they behaved with others. Authoritarianism continued to function as a guide for their own behavior. The exercise of power is still considered the most advisable way to tackle relationships with others, especially in moments of argument or disagreement (Araujo 2016). This is an area that I will explore when discussing irritations. For the moment, I will pause to consider a second dimension of disenchantment with the promise of democratization.

3.2.2 Merit

My work has shown that merit has become an essential element of people's feelings of justice. This should not be read solely as a result of the neoliberal push for success and personal effort – that is, within the framework of meritocracy. The promise of merit reverberates in Chile as a tool, legitimized by the principle of equality, against the reign of the logic of privilege and naturalized hierarchy. For example, it provides a way out of a social world that has historically tended to counter the action of these two logics by mobilizing informal resources of influence, *pitutos* (well-placed contacts), to get a job or a medical appointment, which in turn establishes new privileges (Barozet 2006). Thus, a belief in merit can be read as a promise of democratization of opportunities and rewards, and as the access route to a recognition of one's own merit – something rarely present in individuals' experience, especially of those in the popular sectors (Araujo and Martuccelli 2012).

But everyday experiences showed Chileans that the promise of merit also remained unfulfilled. The argument of a woman from the middle class expresses it well: "For example, if we were all friends and you were promoted to general manager, I mean we are all protected. Whether or not we produce results" (Inv. 1). Even having merit ("doing a good job") in the rarefied and barely transparent world of work could turn out to have negative repercussions. In the words of an upper-middle-class business manager, displaying merit could be negative because it would make you too expensive for the company or very "risky for someone within the system" (Inv. 2).

Despite the promise of merit, moreover, people rarely experience recognition of their own merit. This is a frustration that has been identified in several studies of the Chilean workplace (Stecher, Godoy, and Aravena 2020).

A final piece of evidence of the broken promise of merit is the fact that networks and influence continue to be active and effective. A very large number of people interviewed in one of my studies (Inv. 2) spontaneously acknowledged having made use of *pitutos* recently.

3.3 Disenchantments and the Social Bond

This gap between promises and experiences has had important consequences. Of course, the problem is not the existence of this discrepancy. For example, the promises made by a normative principle, such as equality, are fundamentally an orientation and an impulse to work toward the realization of an ideal. It is impossible to expect a perfect crystallization of the normative principle because this crystallization is nothing more than an effect, always precarious, of the permanent conflicts that take place in a community (Rancière 1995). Reality never corresponds exactly to what the promises of equality or welfare produce in the imagination of each person and in that of the collective. However, the magnitude of the gap between them can vary, and this magnitude is never trivial with regard to people's judgments, attachments to, or rejections of their own society.

The experience of broken promises has produced in Chile a rich vein of disenchantment, some of which we have described in this section. It is the basis of a very critical vision of the social world, its institutions and actors. But it is also at the root of a disbelief: in the words of the participants, there exists a widespread conviction that the promises of society are "*a tremendous fallacy.*" In turn, this leads to a breakdown in the credibility of institutions, of people, and of society itself.

A fission occurs in the social bond when the relationship to normative ideals is established on the basis of mistrust, impotence, or, in an even more worrying version, radical rejection. Citizen engagement – a condition for the stability and strengthening of democracies – is then jeopardized.

At the same time, disenchantment has been accompanied by the preservation of practices contrary to the ideals on which individuals built their critical views. The persistence of these practices is due to the fact that experience shows them to be important in facing social challenges. This has created a set of moral contradictions, which, together with disbelief or indignation, have led, as we will see later, to the production of varied forms of detachment.

On the other hand, it is also true that these promises have affected how individuals perceive the social world and their expectations of it. Essentially, the promises encouraged people to question the logics and principles that had historically shaped sociability and the relationships between different social groups, and that had been an instrument for preserving social distances and distinctions (Araujo 2013). In other words, the promises destabilized the modalities that had sustained social relationships and interactions, and thereby affected the aspect of the social bond that relates to coexistence.

Reordering these social principles and logics, then, has ended up being one of the most important tasks that society must face. But this task is challenged by the emergence of a varied collection of irritations in the relationships and interactions that permeate society. It is to this third component of the circuit of detachment that we will turn in the next section.

4 Irritation

The studies carried out in the first decade of the twenty-first century revealed that Chilean society was shot through with a powerful feeling of irritation. It was a society aroused by anger especially, but also a society with a heightened sensitivity to unpleasant affective reactions so that the relationship between stimulus and response frequently seemed excessive. Finally, irritation was expressed in forms of social relations that were charged with friction and in which there was a noticeable deregulation of the use of force (Araujo 2009: 171–194; Araujo and Martuccelli 2012: Vol. II, 101–141). Thus, the malaise that had been detected in the late 1990s (PNUD 1998), and that had long been characteristic of Chilean society, had now given way to irritation. This feature has been gaining ground throughout the past decade. Evidence of it can be found in my studies on the exercise of authority (Inv. 3; Araujo 2016); on the relationship between institutional politics and citizenship (Inv. 7; Araujo 2019a); or on social interactions occurring in the streets of the capital, Santiago de Chile (Inv. 4; Araujo 2019b). Irritation is not only or primarily political, as authors who emphasize this dimension tend to suggest. Rather, it is present in everyday relationships and interactions across the whole of society.

Irritation is detected in anonymous and intimate relationships alike, in both the public and private sphere, in established relationships as well as in instrumental relationships that are episodic and fleeting. They are present at work (with bosses or colleagues), in relationships with neighbors, in interactions on the streets, as well as with actors in institutional politics. While expressions of irritation are varied, they share a common background in the two dimensions of Chile's current historical condition: on the one hand, there is the growing pressure in the country for horizontalization of the social bond, and the resistance it encounters; and, on the other, there is expansion of the "system" or "model," in which the figure of the "enemy" is generalized, the virtue of competition is disseminated, exchange value is prioritized, and people further withdraw from interaction.

In what follows I will first present some of the faces of irritation and its modalities – anger, hyperreactivity, and the deregulated use of force. I will illustrate them with examples of the kinds of relationship in which they appear: in relations with institutions and with anonymous others. I will then present some of the explanatory clues that my studies have suggested regarding this component of the circuit of detachment.

4.1 The Faces of Irritation

4.1.1 Institutions

Irritation directed at institutions is related to moral criticism of the latter. Individuals' experiences of abuse and mistreatment at the hands of institutions serve to justify a fierce rejection of institutions as well as distrust of and animosity toward them.

The experiences I have described of people having to support themselves and their loved ones on their own gave rise to the idea that one could function in the social world without institutions. Whether plausible or not, it was an extremely powerful notion, despite being contradicted by people's own practices and expectations (as seen in the bitter criticism of the state's failings). It also stemmed from experiences linked to the excessiveness that people had to deal with: the usurious department store loans, the mistreatment by the utility companies, or the immoderate demands and low returns in the world of work, to mention just a few. All of this ended up convincing people that they not only should act without institutions but, even more, they should defend themselves against them. This finds expression in the stories people frequently told about their need to develop different defense strategies, often accompanied by feelings of resignation, helplessness, and indignation.

This hypervigilant attitude, expressed as an intense distrust of institutions, has become dramatically more ingrained in recent years: trust in most institutions (church, police, armed forces, government, companies, or political parties) has reached a historic low (Corporación Latinobarómetro 2020). But, even more, these experiences have led to everyday expressions of open hostility toward institutions or their representatives, as the following two cases illustrate.

In my research in the 2000s (Inv. 1 and 2), public health institutions were strongly associated with experiences of abuse and mistreatment. The long waiting times for access to more complex treatments and operations or over-crowded services were part of this perception, but so were experiences of mistreatment in interactions with staff. People felt that public health services systematically exposed them to humiliation and belittlement. For one thing, they had to face a relentless message that the service was a kind of charity to which they should be grateful. For another, they found themselves repeatedly infantilized. Thus, stories abounded about how health personnel, particularly doctors, "told them off" and considered them objects rather than subjects. This testimony of a young working-class man is a case in point: "When you go to the doctor he tells you off, you go to the *Consultorio*[20] and they tell you off, the relationship between the professional world and the poor is like that, it's to put you in your place, it's your ignorance, it's pointing the finger at your ignorance" (Araujo 2009; Inv. 1).[21] The experience of abuse, then, went hand in hand with repressed anger. But this hostility began to be expressed more directly.

In recent years, there has been a sharp increase in attacks on healthcare personnel. Although there are no cross-country studies, a survey conducted by the Association of Zonal General Doctors of the Medical College showed that 76 percent of the doctors and 96 percent of other healthcare professionals had suffered verbal or physical aggression and that 50 percent expressed feelings of insecurity (Gobierno de Chile 2018), which led to the drafting of regulations and a law to prevent such aggression and to provide protection.[22]

Institutional politics is the setting for the second example of irritation with institutions. Between late 2017 and 2018, we carried out a study to explore the relationships between institutional political actors and citizens, as seen from the point of view of the political actors (Inv. 7; Araujo 2019a). We found that local party activists are frequently attacked and confronted by members of the public. Hostility was a constant feature of these interactions. Many of these accounts revealed, for example, that activists, when canvassing during elections, frequently had to endure being called "thieves" or "creeps"; had to resist being insulted and thrown out of public spaces; had to face threats and aggressive gestures; or had to protect themselves from objects people threw at them.

Note that these hostile encounters had nothing to do with disagreement over political positions – the rejection was not based on ideological differences, whether from the left or the right. Underlying the aggression was a rejection of

---

[20] Public primary healthcare facility.

[21] In a study carried out in 2016 by the PNUD (2017), these results were supported using quantitative methods. 41 percent of the those surveyed stated that they had had experiences of abuse during the previous year. Healthcare facilities were the most common places where the abuse occurred, followed by workplaces and out in public, that is, on the streets.

[22] Law 21888 of December 2019.

politicians as such. Here, too, the reasons were linked to abuse and deceit. During hostile encounters, people commonly voiced the complaint that politicians were only interested in people at election time or that they had come only to take advantage of the public. The intensity of the irritation in these encounters is evident from the metaphors that the activists used to refer to themselves in these contacts with the population: they called themselves "resilient" or the "soldiers," the former connoting survival and the latter connoting warfare (Araujo, 2019a).

4.1.2 Anonymous Others

In the case of anonymous others, an expectation of the other's "malignancy" defines these relationships, and irritation is the main characteristic of these contacts. This feature, which we had already identified in some earlier studies, was more pronounced in our more recent research (Inv. 4 and 5). The testimony of an electrician from the popular sectors summarizes the mood of these experiences: "We are all very aggressive," he said, "everyone looks out for themselves, like I want to get this, I want to get there first before he does" (Inv. 5).

A study of interactions in public spaces conducted in 2016 (Inv. 4; Araujo 2019b) showed that the streets were true arenas of everyday aggravation. Of course, the sensation of threat felt especially in poor areas by the presence of crime or drug trafficking was confirmed. But a striking aspect of these findings was the proliferation of rows or scuffles that broke out in such everyday situations as driving a car, being served in a supermarket, or interacting with a taxi driver. The metaphor of the "jungle" was often used, conveying an image of an everyday interactive tension between people who were "strong" and "weak," between pedestrians, between motorists, or between men and women.

The Santiago Metro is perhaps one of the most telling examples of these moments of irritation. It presents an extreme microcosm of this reality.[23] The Santiago Metro has greatly increased its capacity in the last fifteen years. While

---

[23] In my empirical studies, references to the Metro often serve as a metaphor for society. On the one hand, the Metro is viewed as an expression of social inequality and of the treatment received from society. In 2004, a young man from the popular sectors participating in our studies stated: "There are no poor people here. Like we are all going to feel great since in all the media they keep telling us that we are all great, we are the tops in Latin America. I don't know, we arrive here and we see a tremendous metro, but I arrive at the corner of my house and I see three or four kids dumped there. I've known them since they were little kids, and now I see them dumped" (Inv. 4). On the other hand, the Metro is seen as a manifestation of a highly irritated society. Curiously, the 2019 uprising originated with protests over the cost of the Metro fare, and the Metro was a frequent target of violence in the protests. Many stations and metro cars were destroyed or set on fire.

in 2006 it handled 331 million passengers annually, in 2015 the number had increased to 661 million annual trips (Metro de Santiago 2007, 2015). The enlargement of the Metro map meant that more people living in poorly resourced areas had access to the service. But it also meant a very significant increase in density at the busiest times of day. During the so-called peak hours, density reaches six passengers per square meter, twice the level considered tolerable and one of the highest public transit densities in the world (Tirachini, Hensher, and Rose 2013).

At these peak travel times, which coincide with workers' morning or evening commutes, people have to resort to various tactics in the fight for space. Abrasive behavior often borders on, or becomes, actual violence. To cope, people plan meticulous strategies and are forced to make use of their (often physical) power resources. Shoving, elbowing, or even headbutting commonly occur.

People describe these situations, which they experience as undignified, as being "treated like animals." At the same time, however, critics' own behavior in this scenario is hard to distinguish from that of those whom they criticize. Often those who voice stern criticism participate in the insults or scuffles that typically occur in these encounters.

These agonistic interactions in the Metro involve not only a fight for space but also a dispute over privileges in its use, well illustrated by what could be called the "dilemma of the last seat." While the order of seating priority once appeared to be clear (the elderly, pregnant women, and women, in that order), today it is no longer so. Standoffs over seats for the exclusive use of senior citizens and pregnant women, or fights over the expected offer of a seat by young to elderly passengers, for example, can trigger violence, which may even be reported on social networks. At stake in these clashes are very different views about what constitute valid codes of sociability in society.

For many, the Metro, and thus an important part of their encounter with the city, is a punishing experience. It is a vivid expression of the irritations that run through society.

4.2 Factors in Irritation

Having described some of the faces of irritation in Chilean society, I shall now examine factors that might explain this heightened tension in social relations. The factors are certainly very diverse, but my findings suggest at least four that help elucidate the phenomenon.

The first and, perhaps, most obvious factor is the effect of the excessiveness and disenchantment that individuals must face. For many, the exhaustion, tension, or anxiety produced by immoderate demands coarsen relationships with others, either because anger and rage produce symptoms of overexcitation or because, as people say, they "lose patience." Of course, a contributory factor is the effect of the accumulation of inequalities and discriminatory experiences on individuals' vision of society. But irritation also appears to be a correlate of the excessive social ideals that people are driven to embody. The two most important ones, we found, are the ideal of competence and the ideal of self-reliance (affirmed in the concrete experience of having to "scratch oneself with one's own nails," leading to a selfish and overpowering individualism). For example, let us look at the impact of the ideal of competence on relationships at work. One of the findings of the study on the structural challenges that individuals must face in Chilean society (Inv. 2) was the widespread experience of *"chaqueteo"* (maligning) in the world of work. *Chaqueteo* refers to practices in relationships aimed at criticizing a person, questioning their merits, depriving them of recognition or destroying their image. The study showed how *chaqueteo*, without being a new phenomenon in the country, seemed to have intensified in people's perception, due to the effects of a highly flexible and competitive labor market, which accentuated mutual distrust between workers at a moment when they saw themselves as having little collective capacity to make demands. In this context, people seemed to use *chaqueteo* as a weapon for individual advancement (Araujo and Martuccelli 2012: Vol. II, 31–42).

A second factor is extreme sensitivity regarding interactional inequalities, leading to greater awareness of abuse. While this sharper awareness of abuse drives critical denunciation and vindication, it can also encourage irritated and even abusive overreaction toward the other. The presumption that one is being abused or that others are predisposed to abuse one operates as a premise that leads to various kinds of friction. This heightened awareness of abuse is the main ingredient of mistrust.

A third factor has to do with the present moment in time, during which the formulas that govern interactions, legitimacies, and the social rationalities that intersect them are being actively rearticulated. The challenge to the old relational logics that were based on the conception of a naturalized hierarchy and source of privileges – as well as on other logics that established unquestionable prerogatives in the use and exercise of power – has not made them disappear, nor have clear new formulas yet emerged to govern sociability, civility, and the management of power asymmetries. This has resulted in widespread uncertainty about relational codes, which turns each interaction into a potential arena of dispute. What characterizes a time like this, then, is a lack of certainty about what people can legitimately expect regarding the treatment they receive from another, and what they should give to the other depending on the status and social position they temporarily occupy at each relational crossroads. Versions of how to solve these questions proliferate without being consensual and culminate in confrontations in concrete situations. The uncertainty, and the emphasis placed on conflicting normative versions, end up straining relationships and producing abrasive interactions that people perceive as exhausting (Inv. 4, 5, and 6).

A fourth factor is related to the path followed by the four social logics that have historically participated in shaping social interactions, which we described in the previous section. Two of them, naturalized hierarchies and privilege, have been strongly criticized, and this criticism has achieved public and political visibility and relevance. They have been challenged by the pressure for egalitarianism, but also, paradoxically, by two aspects closely linked to the social ideal promoted by the "model": the celebration of merit and the appeal to the self-reliant subject. While it is true that hierarchies and privilege have not disappeared, it has become harder and harder to justify them in the public debate and the force of criticism has sufficed to gradually limit and sanction them. Constant surveillance, with the help of cell phone cameras, feeds the public space with denunciations of practices such as the ill-treatment of beach supervisors using class arguments ("my time is worth more than yours")[24] or clashes over the use of lakesides (which, while being for public use, have tended to be privatized de facto).[25] These complaints tend to have repercussions and elicit resounding social sanctions.

The other two social logics encountered – authoritarianism and the exercise of power – have become more paradoxical. Although criticism of both, and particularly of authoritarianism, has increased, they have become more prevalent across society. This is especially true of the logic of the exercise of power.

Thus, a study on the exercise of authority in Chilean society (Inv. 3; Araujo 2016) provided evidence of a reappraisal of what constitutes a justifiable exercise of power and widespread criticism of authoritarianism, the customary and historical form the exercise of power has taken in the country. Authoritarianism has two central features. First is the mobilization of implicit coercive resources when exercising authority. As Pamela, a journalist interviewed for this study, put it: "Obey or . . . [claps one hand against the other] a punishment, a reprimand or something negative is implicit."

Second is the expectation that the other must proffer "mechanical obedience," which is based on a modality of exercising authority that assumes a tutelary relationship with "subordinates," curbing their scope for autonomy.

---

[24] www.elmostrador.cl/dia/2021/03/03/yo-te-pago-el-suelo-mujer-responde-molesta-ante-peticion-de-colocarse-mascarilla-en-zapallar/.

[25] www.latercera.com/nacional/noticia/donde-esta-limite-bien-uso-publico-la-propiedad-privada-los-lagos/519028/.

As one interviewee said: "You have to obey because you are no good for anything else, that is just what you have to do" (Inv. 3). However, we also found that this criticism was accompanied by the judgment that authoritarianism was the only efficient way to procure obedience. Moreover, we found that there was a tendency to use the term "authoritarianism" as a synonym for authority. Because authoritarianism is a vector of widely shared criticism, the idea of authority was difficult for them to discern, recognize, and justify. Dismissing authority by confusing it with authoritarianism makes its exercise difficult even in nonauthoritarian forms; that is, it even destabilizes more democratic attempts to exercise authority.

The persistence of authoritarianism is connected to what has happened to the logic of the exercise of power. The confrontational use of power and the ability to impose upon others are considered by many to be essential ways of coping with social life (Inv. 1, 2, and 5). This social logic has been enhanced in recent decades by the ideal of competitiveness, the primacy of exchange value, and the presumption of abuse and its correlate, distrust. This is linked to a perception of society as a complex web of powers whose exercise is unregulated; to a society that conceives of power as a source of abuse and humiliation and therefore as a factor in the erosion of social life, and yet at the same time considers power the most important resource to achieve goals, protect oneself from others, and access resources. Society, as a young man told us, "is a war of power." (Inv. 1; Araujo 2009: chap. 2, 3, and 7). In such a context, the possibility of more egalitarian relationships is weakened because signs of horizontality tend to be read as signs of weakness (Araujo 2016).

In short, based on what we have seen, society appears as a battlefield on which, with no consensus as to what constitutes a legitimate exercise of power, all exercises of power, except one's own, come under suspicion. Thus, if the processes that we have been studying have helped erode the conventional ways in which asymmetries of power were managed in social life, they have not yet provided new ways of solving this problem. In this context, the perception of social life as antagonistic in nature appears to be widely shared and the "law of the jungle" makes inroads among a society of strengthened individuals (Araujo 2019b). Irritation settles in and expands.

5 Detachment

5.1 A Definition

Detachment is the final component of the circuit that comprises different manifestations of excessiveness in the structural demands expressed in everyday challenges; of disenchantment with material promises but also with promises of the democratization of social relations; and of multiple expressions of irritation both with institutions as well as between individuals.

By "detachment" I mean an irregular and multiform process of estrangement and disengagement from the principles, rationalities, and legitimacies that order the social bond. Detachment is associated with a loosening of the links that bind us to society and the common life and with a loss of synchronization with the customary relational modalities and mechanisms that make social coexistence possible. Detachment, crucially, is an active current in society that cuts across all social groups. The concept does not describe a consolidated state of society, nor does it affect the society as a whole. It has several modalities and it does not affect all spheres of social life uniformly. However, it does affect the notion of "the collective" and therefore that of "the common."

Unlike the notion of anomie, as used by Durkheim (1979), the condition I seek to describe is not the inability of shared norms to regulate individual desires and aspirations but, rather, a situation in which individuals feel disenchanted and oppressed by the excessive demands of social life, by the daily irritation it causes, and by the broken promises regarding the norms governing relationships; a situation, moreover, in which individuals have internalized the conviction that solutions must be individual. Detachment, thus, is an individual solution to protect oneself and respond to the harshness of social life, which can take various forms.

In this sense, Robert Merton's version of anomie (1938) also does not apply to the phenomenon I am seeking to describe. Merton derives his approach from a Parsonian reading of Durkheim and focuses on a type of anomie that he attributes to a lack of correspondence between the cultural ends promoted and the legitimate means to obtain them, an analysis he used to critique the culture of success in American society. In detachment, the disjunction between means and ends is not always or necessarily the central issue. Instead, what we are concerned with is the fear or conviction that one must defend oneself and keep one's distance from institutions and others, such that one prefers a degree of social isolation. In this sense, this phenomenon would be closer to "retreatism," one of the responses to anomia identified by Merton, but by no means involving the complete abandonment of society that the author considers definitive of this response.[26] Detachment supposes a type of retreatism that does not imply wholesale disaffiliation from society.

---

[26] For Merton, there are several responses to the situation of anomie. *Conformity* is usually construed as being the absence of anomie (both cultural ends and means are accepted). The other responses are *innovation* (cultural ends are accepted but illegitimate means are used to obtain them), *ritualism* (cultural ends are abandoned but conventional means are followed ritualistically), *retreatism* (both ends and means are rejected as in the extreme case of those who are in society but are not of society), and *rebellion* (both ends and means are rejected and their substitution is sought) (Merton 1938: 676–679).

Detachment not only refers to the regulatory norms of society but also has consequences for the forms of bonding. Contra Durkheim's separation of the two ideas (anomie would explain the lack of normative regulation and egoism would explain the quality of the bond), the phenomenon of detachment throws light on the intimate relationship between both phenomena. It helps to delineate the contours of the two faces of the social bond.

In describing the quality of adherence to the idea of society or "the commons," detachment cannot be reduced to an effect of egoism. That the solutions we find in detachment are individual in nature cannot necessarily be taken to mean a disregard for others. In this sense, detachment does not correspond to the situation of moral anarchy described by Buchanan (1986). But what characterizes these "others" is that they belong to "proximity groups." They feature a strong concern and availability for the other, but only if the other has some characteristic that defines them as close (e.g., they think alike; share filial sentiments or friendship affects).

In regard to the social bond that involves the quality of *regulation*, detachment describes a difficulty in articulating forms of action and evaluation of the principles and logics that underlie those practices. Rather than producing a break with these principles and logics as a whole (although this appears in one of its forms), detachment leads to uncertain, contradictory, or dislocated uses of them and to idiosyncratic formulas for renewal or modification.

Detachment, then, does not refer only to the proliferation of no-go areas (Dahrendorf 1985) – where noncompliance with the norms would be expected – or to a weakening of sanctions. While detachment may take this form, it is not a feature common to all situations. Neither can it be said with any certainty that Chilean society is "on the road to anomia," as Dahrendorf understands it; that is, on a trajectory wherein norms lose validity due to their lack of social efficiency and cultural morality and anarchy ensue from the weakening of authority (1985: 24–26). While this might eventually be an outcome, there is nothing to make it inevitable or even probable. It is not possible today to equate detachment with social disintegration, because detachment can take so many different forms. Detachment does not necessarily imply a break with the principles of coexistence. It does, however, in every case, involve a more or less pronounced distancing from and disaffection with the collective.

While the modalities of detachment are varied, as we will see later, detachment is usually justified on the basis of 1) the exhaustion produced by all the demands of social life, which we have discussed in previous pages, and 2) all the moral criticisms arising from these experiences. Having presented the factors that contribute to detachment, I turn now to the moral critiques that underlie it.

5.2 Moral Reasons for Detachment

As previously discussed, neoliberalism does not entail the suppression of morality but, rather, the fostering of a new morality (Amable 2011; Davies 2014). The transformation of Chilean capitalism did not only involve changes to the economic infrastructure but brought with it a new model of society and of the subject, a set of representations and values that became robust social ideals. The most salient of these, according to research, were the image of a mobile and competitive society; the value attached to personal ambition and individual effort; an image of people as strictly responsible for their own personal fate; and the social value attached to the idea of ownership, all linked to a model of integration via consumption and credit (and not salary). These images imprinted themselves on individuals and institutions (Araujo and Martuccelli 2012).

Following Bourdieu and Foucault, much of the literature on the effects of neoliberalism starts with the idea that its success depends on individuals' adherence to it, which, while neither reflexive nor conscious, is the result of their internalizing or adopting its constraints and values (Bröckling 2017; Dardot and Laval 2009). My findings showed that the case of Chile does not support this assumption. As the neoliberal model and its ideals spread, so did powerful critiques of it, linked to significant moral tensions. As discussed in the previous section, these criticisms were forged by pressures for social democratization, both by the magnifying effect these pressures had on individuals' perceptions of abuses or inequalities and by their contribution to the rhetoric of these criticisms. In most cases, the prevailing perception was not one of adherence but, rather, of the de facto imposition of what study participants called the "system."

Indeed, in two studies – one carried out between 2003 and 2007 (Araujo 2009) and the other between 2007 and 2011 (Araujo and Martuccelli 2012) – we detected a profuse moral criticism of the "system" coming from individuals from very different social and political backgrounds. It had, in fact, become a dominant social interpretation, even among those who had reasons to defend the economic model.

All these criticisms highlighted the excessiveness of the demand to embody the ideals of the subject proposed by the model, due to the moral contradiction that it would entail between the critics' own ideals – which were largely socially active because of the effects of the current of social democratization – and their concrete practices, as well as the widespread moral indolence to which it would have led.

The four main moral criticisms of the model that recur in many different studies (Araujo and Martuccelli 2012: Vol. I, 71–81; Araujo 2009; Inv. 5) are that the model morally erodes society and its individuals because it 1) boosts competition; 2) demands that appearances be kept up; 3) feeds consumerism; and 4) injects materialism into society.

Competition pushes one to be abusive and predatory. This criticism fits with a vision of society as a constant battle of powers. Indeed, according to a survey used to document the social structure in the Metropolitan Region of Santiago, 79.7 percent agreed that the economic system led to competition, making affect and solidarity between people more difficult (Mayol, Azócar, and Azócar 2013). In the words of a postal worker: "why did we come to that, why can't we be happy, why do we have to live so stressed out, causing us so much rivalry, so much selfishness, which is a strong word, that's why I say to be a little more humanitarian, it's hard, it's very hard" (Inv. 5).

Consumerism, for its part, seems to be responsible for having commercial-ized social relations and emptied people of their moral sense. In Chile, "people are very contaminated with the issue of consumerism, they live to work and to consume," a small trader from the popular sectors told us (Inv. 5). It distorts priorities and leads to feelings of emptiness and spiritual impoverishment. But consumerism alters family relationships too. The result is that family demands are structured in those terms, transforming the signs of love and care. Referring to his children, an artisan commented, "it is as if they are born connected with a cable from before birth, they are already connected with a cable, so the bombardment is not controllable" (Inv. 2).

The excessive demand to keep up appearances is evidence of the spread of social pretension and is fuel for inauthenticity. Criticism of the cult of appear-ance cuts across all sectors of society because all have experienced it, whether linked to the recognition of status, especially in the case of the wealthy sectors, or used as a strategy to protect oneself from abuse and discrimination, as in the popular sectors (Araujo 2009). In either case, it promotes superficiality.

Finally, materialism and the dominance of money in defining social value exclude spiritual principles, non-economic considerations, and above all, the ethical dimension of relationships with others. The words of an engineer are illustrative: "We are traitors, we are all scoundrels, we are all mules, and we all go for the money, nothing else, like a bunch of pirates and mercenaries, nothing more . . . like those animal species where the weak are thrown out, cut off from the herd, and die far away" (Inv. 2). Materialism, spiritual emptiness, and a lack of solidarity are frequently linked in this critique.

But, while moral criticism featured constantly in the discourse of individuals, this did not necessarily imply an abandonment of practices that indeed reflected what was so bitterly criticized. The weight of their knowledge of the logics governing social life, distilled from their own experiences, is an important part of the explanation for this. While interviewees felt able to express these criticisms, they understood that there was no way out and that not complying would be too costly for their survival or interests. While the normative ideals that spread during these decades were powerful rhetorical tools to legitimize criticism, they were too weak to fulfill their function of inspiring individual acts (Araujo 2009; Inv. 5).

Under the wing of these ideals, a series of different moral contradictions emerged, when the very practices (competitive, materialistic, etc.) individuals felt compelled to adopt clashed with the social, moral, and sociability values that they considered important. These contradictions persistently distanced individuals from their ideal selves and prevented them from being the kind of people that felt they should be. Both criticisms and contradictions, as we will see, underlie to differing degrees the varieties of detachment described below.

5.3 The Modalities of Detachment

Detachment takes various forms, which reveal the different and contradictory currents running through contemporary Chilean society. In my work, I have found four varieties of detachment: refuge, a new start, apparent adherence, and defiant contempt and the adversarial construction of alternative worlds (Inv. 5). Let us examine each of these in detail.

5.3.1 Refuge

In this version of detachment, neither the normative frame nor the principles of social regulation are actively questioned, but forms of protection are sought in a quest for less-exposed spaces, as if moving from center stage to the wings. Refuge-seekers aim to protect themselves from the relentless coercion of a system that pushes them to their physical and mental brink, or to shelter from the irritation of social relationships. But they also seek to avoid moral contradiction. What they hope to achieve is what many interviewees considered their most important goal: tranquility, which they frequently equated with happiness.

Their criticism does not lead to adversarial expressions but to the search for ways, whether imaginary or real, of protecting themselves. This modality offers another option beyond Hirschman's (1970) famous trio of *exit*, *voice*, and *loyalty*. In a given situation of discontent, actors not only have recourse to strategies of escape (*exit*), protest (*voice*), or adherence (*loyalty*); they may also pursue forms of disengagement or displacement that enable them to remain and support themselves in the same situation in which they find themselves – a sort of attenuated exit strategy. Let us consider a couple of examples.

A first example is provided by one of the findings of a study of how individuals support themselves when facing the social challenges that they encounter (Inv. 5). One of the most important existential anchors individuals mentioned, and by far the most common, was to cherish an expectation of moving in the future to the south (an area of the country featuring forests, lakes, and rivers, linked to representations of human warmth and natural beauty) or to the countryside. This expectation for the future appeared both as a desire and as the outline of a plan (Araujo 2018).

This expectation expressed individuals' hope of one day being able to leave behind the need to be competitive, aggressive, and indifferent, or the need to deal with the irritations that arise in daily encounters with others. It expressed the dream of not having to raise children with the threat of crime and drugs and of not having to respond to the requirements of appearance. The south and the countryside appeared as imaginary spaces where there would be a greater experience of humanity (kindness, slower rhythms, courtesy) and where longed-for tranquility, the opposite of excessiveness, would be found. This expectation runs across social sectors and is not restricted to inhabitants of the capital, although it is found only in urban areas. Those who live in smaller cities also dreamed of leaving them for a life in more protected (rural) areas. For example, a woman named Oriana, from the capital, believed that she could find in the countryside "the simplicity of the people, the humility of the people" that does not exist in Santiago. Pedro, a resident of a coastal provincial city, considered that in the countryside people were less envious, happier, more loving, and more receptive, so that there one could relax the attitude of constant vigilance and distrust that, in his view, characterized his everyday experience.

A second example of this modality of detachment is the extremely wide-spread desire to work for oneself. While for some, self-employment is an expectation for the future, for others it is a current reality. In many cases, it is an activity conducted in parallel with formal wage labor. In other cases, self-employment is a present or past stage of a career path whose stability cannot be guaranteed.[27] The concrete realities are multiple, but what is central is its significance and its use to support oneself in social life. In the great majority of cases, this form of work is viewed as desirable or, more strictly, as preferable. People invest in the idea of self-employment their hopes of leading more livable

---

[27] According to the National Socioeconomic Characterization Survey of 2015, 19.2 percent of workers were self-employed. It is a segment that is growing and is the second most important group in the Chilean labor market. The precarity of self-employment can be seen from the fact that 50 percent of the self-employed have a monthly income of less than CLP 200,000 (Venegas 2017), which is less than USD 300.

lives, even though self-employment is regarded not only by experts but by the individuals themselves as highly risky, poorly protected, and vulnerable.

The appeal of self-employment is related to the excessive personal toll of wage labor. A study carried out with self-employed workers from popular sectors (Venegas 2017) found that salaried employment was associated with a lack of recognition. The demanding nature of salaried employment and the lack of control over their time interfered with individuals' ability to respond to family demands, and exposed workers to arbitrary and abusive treatment by bosses as well as to management irrationality. In this context, working for oneself was recognized as being more demanding, with a greater burden of insecurity and precarity, but it was viewed as a route to recovery from moral damage, a path to personal dignity, and a way of gaining control over one's time.

For those who did not harbor dreams of escaping to the south or to the countryside, the hope of future self-employment and independence acted as an existential anchor. Unable to completely abandon the world of work, their only option was to protect themselves from what they considered the greater evil, which is, paradoxically, to fend off the harshness of dependent jobs. Refuge is a form of detachment that opts for retreat or displacement, whether real or imaginary, toward what might be called "shielded zones."

5.3.2 The New Start

This modality of detachment has several points in common with that of refuge. It also aims for protection against the excessive demands of social life and, like the quest for refuge, aspires to the ultimate state of tranquility. It differs from refuge, however, in that it involves active ways of constructing alternatives.

Protection here is not conceived as a mere blanket but is thought of as integral to the construction of other worlds and actively involving other subjects. Its key content is the transformation of lifestyles. This modality places the potential for change at its center. It produces finished versions of a new world that are able to defeat the demands of a system that imposes highly competitive attitudes, tensions between different spheres of life (such as work and family), or neglect of what for many people are the most important source of meaning: children. It is not, however, about changing the social world or combating the lifestyles of others. It is about the nonadversarial construction of alternative worlds: finding spaces, whether relational or geographical, that make it possible to change oneself and one's way of living.

Let us return to the case of the south and the countryside as expectations for the future to illustrate this type of detachment. If some of my interviewees associated going to the south or to the countryside with the idea of refuge, others did so with the idea of making a new start in life. Perhaps a good way to illustrate the distinctiveness of the latter position is to compare how these expectations are described by two of my interviewees. In the refuge mode, a young entrepreneur, a naval engineer, said that he had the idea with his wife to go south, but to be "calm, alone, in our world." In the new start mode, a health professional told of her dream plan of going to the south with her partner to start a small organic farming business that would allow them to have a different relationship with nature and with themselves. The new start modality occurred particularly in young adults from the well-off middle classes. Two factors – stage of life and available material resources – contributed to aspirations for the future, which were presented in the form of a pilot plan in these cases. Nevertheless, the dream cuts across social sectors. It is well illustrated by the observation of an owner of a coffee shop in his fifties who, with great admiration, said that more and more young people were doing what he would have liked to have done but could not do now, owing to his age and responsibilities: "They are going to live in towns, they are leaving the city, they don't want to be city dwellers; they want to make a change, starting by changing their lives."

In these cases, moral criticism was sharper and more organic, and the value, emotional, and affective dimensions were of the greatest importance. This alternative world also had as its main constituent the adoption of more natural, slower, more strenuous, less well-paid, but ultimately happier ways of living; a world in which a different relationship with nature, stemming from increased awareness of and concern for the environment, was a frequent and widespread feature. This new start would allow them more time for themselves and their significant others; help them create new forms of relationship with their surroundings; enable them to be more responsible for the fate of the environment; allow the cultivation of new values such as empathy and solidarity; and make it possible to live with fewer moral contradictions and, therefore, to live a more authentic life. A 47-year-old researcher and university lecturer in the area of natural sciences, who also hoped to go south one day, had as a model some "schoolmates who live supporting themselves in the countryside ... they eat what they plant, and they bring up and educate their children, and the only thing they have electricity for, with these solar things, is to connect to the internet once a week and for their cell phones" (Inv. 5).

The south and the countryside appeared, then, as spaces that could be turned into the setting for a new lifestyle. The new start refers to a world that they would participate in creating by transforming themselves: a substantial change that demands new performances.

The modalities of the new start and refuge have in common the effect of weakening the density of links with global society. Both involve a strategy, whether imaginary or real, of moving toward the edges, distancing themselves from what they imagine to be the central nucleus of society. Ultimately, their motivation is the construction of protected worlds. Both cases involve individual responses or include, at most, the forging of links with very restricted "proximity groups," thus narrowing the extent of the shared world. Neither case involves a radical break with the normative foundations of the social order itself. But, in the modality that we have just analyzed, all this is also linked with sharp moral criticism, a longed-for change of personnel, and the consistent replacement of a selected set of social values and relational principles that they perceive as erosive for them and their lives.

5.3.3 Apparent Adherence

In this modality, unlike the previous two, there is no exit strategy. Apparent adherence is more about permanence. It is a case of staying and doing what needs to be done, for which one must know very well how things work and take advantage of all the opportunities that come one's way, while mobilizing an ideal and edifying discourse that takes the form of moral criticism of the social world (Inv. 1; Araujo 2009; Inv. 5).

In this modality, escape from "the system" is viewed as impossible. The "system" is criticized in a condemnatory and even bitter tone, accompanied by exacting moral judgments, but given that one is obliged to remain in "the system" and no exit is possible, one determines to extract as much benefit as possible from the situation. Thus, all one's skills and abilities are deployed not only to successfully pass the tests one must face but also to benefit as much as possible in each situation. Thus, social life is approached by seeking in each situation to extract an advantage or limit a disadvantage. Hence the paradoxical mixture of pragmatism, idealism, and instrumentalization that accompanies this modality of detachment.

Also, unlike in other modalities, in apparent adherence individuals do not seek to avoid moral contradictions but, rather, to learn to live with them. This requires a complex task of self-justification or, simply, dissociative formulas that allow criticism to continue to be expressed while simultaneously practicing what is criticized.

It is a form of detachment that is also individual, like refuge, but exists on a mass scale in society. It is individual because it requires especially demanding personal performances, but also because, given the contradiction it entails, it cannot be explicitly collectivized. It is massive because it literally cuts across all social groups. This has very important effects. It enables one to feel excused because its widespread presence suggests that "everybody does it." At the same time, it naturalizes the situation so that many are simply not aware of the moral contradiction on which they base their lives.

There is an accommodation to the world order, but this is practiced while affirming disbelief in the principles that govern its practices, and at a practical distance, given the social criticism expressed. This combination leads to the generation of a distanced relationship with the set of principles that order social life, and with the collective. It is a reading in a strongly individual code, however collective the critical rhetoric may be. Detachment from the collective correlates with a way of evaluating the events of the social world that has the individual as the reference point, and that focuses on the advantages and disadvantages of these events for the individual. Their attachments to the social order are weak, changeable, and feigned.

5.3.4 Adversarial Alternatives

The last type of detachment involves a more extreme form of disengagement. It presupposes the generation of alternative worlds that are based on a rejection of society and a confrontation with its principles, logics, and rationalities. These adversarial forms have been comprehensively studied by the social sciences in two of their versions: normative orders that function outside and in opposition to the law, and movements to transform and radically change societies. But this modality can also be found in a less extreme and more everyday version that cannot be explained by theories of marginality or criminality, nor by political theories. While this phenomenon is not recent, it is current and is spreading. To discuss it, I will refer to the results of a study of the relationship between normative principles and action orientation carried out in the early 2000s (Inv. 2).

My findings showed, as I have already discussed, that the contradictions between social promises and ordinary experiences had given rise to various types of disenchantment. But they also showed that one of the potential effects of disenchantment was a distancing from the rules and norms that are considered politically, legally, and civilly to be the basis for the regulation of living alongside others. In addition, this disenchantment led to the idea that the orientation and regulation of action was the individual responsibility of each person and not of some type of collective consensus. There was a fission effect, to use a concept from physics. The effect was defiance and contempt for authority and the adversarial construction of alternative spaces, starting either from a displacement toward the margins or from the very "center" of society.

Placing yourself on the margin is linked to a selective compliance with the rules as necessary to survive in the social world. On this point, as in the case of apparent adherence, a quota of pragmatism is present, but it is used minimally. What characterizes adversarial alternatives as a modality is withdrawal to a space that is conceived as governed by arbitrary will. Its consequences are irony and the radical questioning of any authority or of the legitimacy of rules: contempt, as in "the law is me."

Doing so, from the "centre of society" involves, just as in the case of apparent adherence, rather than a general questioning of the normative order, its factual erosion accompanied by its rhetorical maintenance. However, unlike in the former, here there is an active distortion and arbitrary application of the rules and regulations for one's own benefit, an aspect neatly conveyed by the phrase "I am the law."

In the phrase "the law is me" (I give myself the law), the general normative order is undermined. It has suffered a kind of implosion due to social experience. Distrust, the conviction that the order of law is a mere tool for abuse, radical distance, and placing oneself on the margin lead to this position. As a young adult from the popular sectors commented: "I, I don't know, at this point . . . I take a totally anti position, I don't accept this system, this model, in fact, I don't vote, all the same I can't stay out of everything. But OK, if there are no rights, you have to take hold of your own things as you like, it doesn't matter to me."

"I am the law" refers to the identification of the law with the individual or group that it represents. In the name of the law, legal principles or other principles of social regulation are distorted and a corrupt use is made of them. A collapse of the principles that order coexistence has not yet occurred, but practices contribute to their frequent temporary suspension. This happens because people consider that the normative regulation is ineffective so they are obliged to take the law into their own hands. As a young person from the popular sectors said, "It's like, because with the law it can't be done, you have to do it yourself." Temporary suspension of law-abiding behavior also occurs because people seek to game the system for personal benefit. In my studies, this last form appeared strongly linked to institutions or collectives. Belonging to a collective authorizes this identification between the ego and the social law that makes its arbitrary and even abusive use possible. An example is the story of a young man detained by the police, who falsely accused him of alcohol consumption to punish him for not behaving with due respect for authority. Another more recent example is the expansion of *funas* (demonstrations of repudiation against a person or group, conceived as an act of justice) by different movements or social groups. While this modality does not imply a desire to permanently place oneself on the margins of society, each temporary suspension of legal principles further marginalizes them.

In any of its versions, this modality of adversarial alternatives involves the most determined withdrawal from the common world and a fundamental questioning of the principles of social coexistence.

———

The four modalities of detachment involve different degrees of distance and disaffection from the principles, rationalities, and logics that organize social relations and interactions. However, what this discussion has shown is that most of the modalities do not involve a radical break. The first three (refuge, new start, and apparent adherence) involve a relationship of selective acceptance or rejection rather than a radical break, and they have very little stability. The final modality involves a more radical and global rejection of the normative framework, as well as forms of its arbitrary use that amount to real but temporary personal normative universes that affect the relational framework and have powerfully erosive effects on the principles and logics that govern them.

Beyond this difference, however, all these modalities of detachment help weaken a more integral vision of the collective. This is not, of course, because of the criticism they mobilize, since this could be considered a motive for change in a situation that they find oppressive, but because each of them reveals the effects of a form of individualism that is expressed in thinking about social life as highly individualistic, including, at most, considerations about "proximity groups." This is, to some degree, a corporate relationship to social life.

All four modalities are erosive insofar as they place people imaginatively outside of society, that is, outside its center. This contributes to the virtual absence of an idea of the common that is recognized for its complexity and diversity. What is shared in these modalities tends to be limited to those who are "like oneself."

At the same time, all the modalities help reduce the intensity of the bond with society. None of the modalities contains elements that identify with society as a whole. They start from the conviction that society is incapable of offering those elements of identity that help satisfy individuals' need for dignity.

Finally, it is worth noting that these modalities do not involve a widespread transgression of norms that is upheld as the acceptable form of collective action. Except in the modality of adversarial alternatives, there is no fundamental questioning of what is minimally necessary to make social coexistence possible. As we have emphasized, what is revealed is the selectivity and arbitrariness that characterizes individuals' relationship with norms and principles.

6 The Circuit of Detachment and the Political Bond

The components of the circuit that we have described – excessiveness, disenchantment, irritation, and detachment – must be seen as acting synchronically. This synchronicity is key to understanding Chilean society today. A set of phenomena that we think of as contradictory or simply illegible are, strictly speaking, the result of the plurality of currents in action. This simultaneity also contributes to the high levels of uncertainty in which social life must develop today. The circuit of detachment weakens individuals' adherence to society and drastically changes their relationship with the principles of action and ideals that used to order social relations and interactions. A fission occurs when one's relationship with society, its institutions, and individuals is based on mistrust, on the need to take a protective step back, or, even more worryingly, on radical rejection. Whether an engaged citizenry is a condition for societal stability remains an open question, but the social and political bonds seem to be on shaky grounds.

6.1 Detachment and the Political Bond

Detachment cannot be treated as equivalent to political disaffection. Detachment does not entail a definitive withdrawal from politics, but it does indicate that individuals' relationships with politics have become much less ideologically or organizationally coherent.

In the case of Chile, although the neoliberal project was initially quite successful in promoting popular political demobilization (Kurtz 2004), it paradoxically led over time to an increase of popular political mobilization (Arce and Bellinger 2007). In particular, neoliberalism displaced the traditional forms in which political mobilization had been organized with a more diverse spectrum of actors and political tactics (Roberts 2008). All of this happened alongside a serious erosion of institutional politics (Luna 2017; Bargsted and Somma 2018) in a country characterized by what Albertus and Menaldo (2018) have called an elite-biased democracy. This explains, for example, why there is no contradiction between the expanding process of detachment and the social uprising of 2019.

In fact, the circuit of detachment reveals how the processes that frame this moment of Chilean history contributed to institutional erosion but have not necessarily weakened the political agency of individuals. Along with a growing disenchantment and irritation that has fueled a perception of institutions as sources of threat and disappointment, individuals, as I have pointed out, have gained more confidence in their own abilities and capacities to make their way in the world. They have increased their demands for autonomy but in the context of the heightened value attached to individuality and individual solutions. Strengthened individuals and the questioning of institutions characterize the present situation. As has been pointed out, a lack of individuals' compliance weakens institutions and weak institutions are a potential threat to democracy (Brinks, Levitsky, and Murillo 2019), but this lack also threatens societies themselves (Martuccelli 2021).

Of course, institutional politics is particularly affected by this situation. As my latest studies show (Inv. 4, 5, and 8), individuals tend to consider themselves morally superior to institutions, which, in their view, are made up of corrupt congressmen, parties guided by private interests, and so on. They develop irritated ways of relating to institutional actors and of judging them. Additionally, most individuals tend not to recognize political actors as genuine authorities and may even consider institutional politics expendable. In a study of the exercise of authority (Inv. 3), I asked my interviewees to name a true authority figure. Very few of them named a politician. A significant percentage of respondents initially declared they couldn't identify a true authority figure in the Chilean public sphere. Many of them, in fact, named family members, such as their mothers or fathers. Moreover, the growing importance of self-orientation and self-regulation (linked to the importance of the principle of autonomy and the expansion of new technologies) weakens the idea that politicians or those linked to social morality are needed to provide guiding ideas and to translate them into lines of action in individuals' everyday lives.

Yet, it is imperative to stress that all the above does not necessarily lead individuals to abandon politics in the broader sense of the term. They have too long a list of things they want to see changed. They still direct their demands to the institutions and have learned in the past decade, thanks to the successes of mobilizations such as those of university students in achieving concrete changes,[28] that improvements can be effected through political action. Obviously, this does not mean that they believe they should therefore get fully involved with the institutional dynamics of politics. Many abstain from electoral politics or renounce institutional politics for reasons as diverse as passive indifference or outright rejection, as in the case of some strands of detachment that involve adversarial alternatives. But above all, detachment neither manifests itself in a single way nor does it entail a complete break. Rather, it leads to highly selective forms of involvement, which tend to be specific, are rarely institutionalized, and are guided by an evaluation of situations in which the main criterion is how they affect the actor in individual terms, even if their justifying rhetoric refers to collective issues (Inv. 5).

---

[28] For a discussion of the true scope of these achievements, see Penaglia and Mejías (2019).

Nevertheless, this circuit does pose serious challenges to institutional politics. To face the circuit of detachment, the latter must reconstruct, almost from scratch, the way it engages the individuals whom it addresses. As I have argued, these are strengthened individuals who disbelieve institutions, are suspicious of mediations, are sensitive to how they are treated, have high and specific expectations, and are highly emotional. At the same time, institutional politics must find ways to establish links with an *archipelago society*. Because of various factors exacerbated by detachment, society has come to resemble a group of islands that, despite their differences, appear gathered in configurations that are a product of their proximity rather than the existence of a common substratum.

6.2 Political Tasks in the Era of Detachment

How does one undertake these political tasks in the era of detachment; that is, in a society of strengthened individuals living in an archipelago society? It is of course difficult to give a definitive answer, but perhaps it is possible to extract some clues from what I have presented so far. Let me mention four.

6.2.1 The Understanding of the Relationship between Society and Politics

To begin with, politics, its actors and analysts, need to draw more attention to the fate of the social bond itself. The relationship between society and politics can no longer be approached without making thorough use of the keys to the social processes that run through the former and also, it is worth remembering, the actors of the latter. Both the individuals who are engaged with politics and the political actors themselves are influenced by the forms the social bond takes in a society. For example, in Chile, the structural transformations of recent decades have changed society and its individuals in terms of their expectations, demands, judgments, value hierarchies, and self-image. This has had enormous consequences for the practice of democracy. As my studies have shown, this transformation has altered what Chileans demand from political actors. The manner of treatment, the management of hierarchies, and the leveling of relationships are among the elements that must be considered in defining what it is to act democratically within a political culture that, in the view of Chileans, was for too long characterized by vertical, authoritarian, elitist, and tutelary kinds of relationship (Araujo 2016). Similarly, the language of abuse and disrespect has become the usual expression for what people increasingly perceive to be the result of politically and morally intolerable attitudes. Abusive behavior fuels a sense of lack of public and political legitimacy and is often used as an argument for disobedience.

Consider, for example, the following insight gained from my previous studies. As I have discussed, Chileans' contemporary everyday experiences have become one of the most important compasses to guide their behavior, their judgments about society, and their adherence to or rejection of social ideals. This applies also to their relationship with politics and political actors. This is probably one of the most radical consequences (and signs) of how much weaker the metanarratives offered by politics have become, and of how misplaced is the conviction that they are capable of shaping societies. The evidence shows that people increasingly base their judgments and ways of behaving on their common and everyday experiences, and not on grand frames of meaning. Without a doubt, this is a basic element underlying global phenomena such as the loss of trust in institutions, the expansion of post-truth, or the gradual migration to social networks as the preferred source of information. Just as happens with other social spheres, people judge politics and politicians based on their everyday profiles and are influenced more by concrete experiences than by elaborate speeches or abstract notions. Political actors are judged less on the basis of their grand achievements than on the basis of their tiny actions. Simple everyday exemplarity, whatever the political ideology or the political positioning, has made itself a central element in political actors' ability to engage individuals. The capacity to connect with basic everyday experiences is one of the most important tools for obtaining support from the electorate or for accomplishing political identification.

In summary, processes at the level of the social bond take precedence over those at the political level, a reversal of the way in which this relationship was traditionally conceived.

6.2.2 The Social Meaning of Institutional Politics

Another essential question concerns the meaning that institutional politics and its actors have for society today.

In Chile's case, this question has been clouded by the political world's insistence on strategies defined by electoral rhythms, timing, and demands. A study I carried out on the relationship between institutional politics and society (Inv. 7) showed that party activists, especially young people, were aware that this primacy of the electoral dimension of politics was one of the reasons for the hostility they encountered in their interactions with people. In fact, as activists of different political parties told us (Inv. 7), one of the important things they had to learn when campaigning is how to be "tough" enough to resist constant verbal – and even sometimes physical – aggression. They had to learn to endure being called "corrupt," "thieves," or "criminals," or how to dodge the fruit thrown at them in popular sector outdoor markets. A reason frequently given for this aggression or rejection was, according to these activists, people's claim that politicians appeared in their neighborhoods only at election time, abandoning the population the rest of the time.

With politicians distant from their constituencies, with no lasting presence to build ties and trust and no everyday experience of local realities to serve as a sounding board, politics have increasingly become a purely transactional matter of supply and demand rather than a source of visions for the future, able to provide images of a desirable, achievable, and common future that could challenge society. Without political actors present in their territories, individuals started to see politics as an abstract and distant phenomenon, just at the moment when everyday experience had become their lodestone for finding their bearings in the social and political world. Electoral politics only increases the distance, because it loses sight of its central task in societies like Chile affected by the circuit of detachment – namely, to give purpose to its existence by defending the relevance of its role for society and individuals. The common accusation that politics is an activity involving purely personal or corporate interests is often nothing more than an expression of the difficulty people have in explaining to themselves convincingly why politics and politicians should continue to exist.

6.2.3 Polarized Ways of Representing Conflict

Another way to face detachment would be to cease contributing to an antagonistic vision of society through polarized ways of representing conflicts. A polarized vision is nothing new in the country. Despite changes to the nature of Chilean society, the right–left polarization (between prodictatorship and antidictatorship, or the more brutal one of *comunachos* vs. *fachos*)[29] remains an important element in structuring relations between groups and individuals (Hunneus 2003). It functions as the basic criterion for differentiation, which cuts across all socioeconomic groups. A second type of polarization finds expression in a class antagonism that can be characterized, somewhat simplistically, as that of "the rich" vs. "the poor" (Araujo 2009). A third, more recent type of polarization is linked to a logic of competition in which individuals picture themselves in a zero-sum struggle for opportunities (Inv. 5). Thus, the tendency to polarize accounts of conflict perpetuates the country's divided character and its tendency to turn conflicts into dead-end confrontations.

---

[29] A colloquial shorthand for communists and fascists. From the 1988 plebiscite that ended Pinochet's dictatorial regime to the present, the use of this trope has been prominent in every electoral campaign, including in the most recent presidential campaign of 2021.

Institutional politics, by reinforcing this tendency, is digging its own grave. Polarization, while it may succeed in gaining votes, deepens detachment. Hence, it serves short-term electoral goals while at the same time eroding long-term political stability. Why?

It is well known that polarization discourages democratic, peaceful ways of representing and managing conflict (Levitsky and Ziblatt 2018). It also simplifies complex political issues (Innerarity 2020) by framing political problems as conflicts between binary opposites. But polarization has more than procedural consequences; it also deepens detachment. It weakens the idea of the common by limiting the notion of the collective to people who are like oneself. It strengthens a notion of the collective built upon "proximity" criteria. Conflicts appear as mere dead-end confrontations, thereby brutalizing social life and contributing to the perception of society as a source of harshness and to a perception of the other as above all a source of threat and irritation. Hence, polarization deepens the search for distance and protection from society, but also from politics itself. That is how politics can ultimately erode the conditions of its own survival.

There is yet another reason politics should not encourage this radical disjunctive form of conflict. In this polarized scenario, political actors are the first candidates to be viewed as the enemy. After all, for many people, excessiveness and disenchantment are intimately linked to the political class's desertion of its role in protecting the population.

6.2.4 Politics and Authority

The circuit of detachment poses an extremely important challenge to the exercise of political authority. It is not only a pragmatic issue but also a normative one. It addresses the very important issue of how to govern archipelago societies with strengthened individuals. In other words, it addresses the urgent problem of social regulation. Let us take a closer look at this problem.

A very important trait of current Chilean society is an ambivalent process concerning the exercise of authority (Araujo 2016a). On the one hand, there is an extended questioning of and critical rupture with the elitist, authoritarian, and tutelary model of social relations. Abuse by the powerful, mistreatment from elites who insist on their "natural" superiority, the exclusion actively displayed by these elites, and the informal networks of influence and power at work in society are all manifestations of the power deregulation Chileans perceive occurring in their society. As we have seen, people consider that they must actively protect themselves from this deregulation. Distancing themselves from institutions or developing forms of detachment are two of the paths that individuals take in the face of this perceived threat. Moreover, people link this deregulation with the way in which relations between the political class and other members of society have traditionally occurred. Although power is perceived, at the same time, as a resource of great value and strong social utility, the ways in which the political class manages power are under constant surveillance. In any case, the "traditional" conception of the exercise of authority, as tutelary and elitist, which was taken for granted as the way one practiced politics in Chile, has become unacceptable to a large segment of the population, especially those who interpret this historical modality as a manifestation of the denial of one's own autonomy.

Second, despite the rejection of authoritarian ways of exercising authority, individuals tend to consider that the strong exercise of authority is necessary to get things done. That is, the form of the exercise of authority they recognize as efficient is precisely the modality that they reject. "Fear of subordinates" is a widespread phenomenon in Chilean society. Whoever exercises authority fears that if you loosen control, subordinates will, for example, abuse your trust or shirk their duties at work. Consequently, large systems of rules, controls, punishments, and threats must be generated. If you do not exhibit strength, you are at risk of having your authority undermined. These fears encourage the maintenance or reinforcement of authoritarian modalities of exercising authority, which encompass political authority.

Conventional political modalities of exercising authority are therefore strongly in tension. If politics is essentially an application of the arts of government, it is these formulas of managing the asymmetries of power that are being questioned in society. But this questioning occurs without new agreements on the possible and acceptable ways of managing these asymmetries. Moreover, questioning coexists with strongly-rooted authoritarian practices. The former leaves the space open to positions ranging from the most anarchic to the most restorative forms of authoritarian exercise of authority. In the turmoil, space is created for the emergence of tendencies toward the abdication of political authority under the influence of a simplistic conception of egalitarianism (which implies a dangerous denial of the power relations that effectively and always exist between all members of society) as well as a disposition toward a rigid authoritarian conception of the exercise of political authority (which threatens basic democratic principles).[30]

---

[30] Belief in the effectiveness of authoritarianism is undoubtedly one of the many factors that explain the outcome of the last presidential election (2021). The extreme right-wing candidate José Antonio Kast made it to the second round of the election. He mobilized the fear of disorder and emphasized his "strong" authority, which allegedly would guarantee success in solving the problems of citizen insecurity, violence, and immigration. Gabriel Boric, a young candidate from the left-wing coalition Apruebo Dignidad won the election. In the second round he had to shift his strategy and made it clear that he would efficiently exercise his authority and pledged to avoid social disorder.

But the scenario is even more worrying. In Chile, authority and authoritarianism are usually regarded as true synonyms. One consequence, as I have just discussed, is the idea that only authoritarianism will achieve obedience. A second consequence is that, due to this equivalence of terms, authority, which is an indispensable phenomenon for social coordination and the management of hierarchies in society, ends up being construed in a way that makes any exercise of authority intrinsically negative and undesirable. This leads to general questioning and distrust of any hierarchy and authority. Detachment is also fed by this disbelief. The very notion of authority ends up falling out of favor. The vicissitudes of political authority are also to be understood from this perspective.

Despite all these challenges, the exercise of political authority is a dimension rarely considered by institutional politics and politicians. There are, without a doubt, and in consideration of the above, various tasks pending in this regard for institutional politics, especially for democratic forces. Today, democratic political forces are impelled to confront the country's elitist, top-down, authoritarian, and tutelary historical tendencies and not abdicate their responsibility to exercise political authority while both challenging and resisting the idea that only an authoritarian form of authority is effective. This is especially important when addressing the circuit of detachment. Durable political attachments and social regulation become more difficult in archipelago societies composed of strengthened individuals. Authoritarianism is always a seductive alternative, even more so when those individuals are torn between their longing for autonomy, their need for protection, and their fear of uncertainty and disorder, as is the case in Chile.

It appears necessary to reinvent the exercise of authority in politics; detachment makes doing so a political moral obligation.

———

Having addressed some of the most salient challenges that the circuit of detachment poses to politics, I conclude in the following section with some brief final reflections on the analytical scope of the concept of the circuit of detachment.

7 Final Reflections

Studies of how structural changes affect individuals and societies have tended to focus on the impact of the so-called neoliberal economic and social model. The results of my research have shown that the neoliberal model, while important, is not the only structural factor to have played a significant role in recent decades. In the case of Chile, and in other Latin American countries (Domingues 2009; Martuccelli 2015), another important structural change is the push for democratization of social relations. The circuit of detachment is the result of the changes these two structural factors have produced in the ordinary challenges people must face in social life and of individuals' responses to these challenges, responses that have included mobilizing support, restructuring one's self-image, modifying ideals, and producing new expectations and practices.

Recognizing that the challenges Chilean society faces result from the interaction of the different components of this circuit made it easier to clarify phenomena that at first appeared paradoxical. For example, I was able to explain the spread of protests and mobilizations against the neoliberal model, as has happened in Chile, not as pure resistance to the effects of a generalized neoliberal subjugation but, rather, as itself a product of these structural currents. Moreover, this recognition allows one to understand the oscillations of the electoral results of the last two years. These have ranged from the massive (78 percent) voter support in October 2020 for changing the constitution promulgated under the Pinochet dictatorship, to 44 percent of voters supporting conservative, strongly neoliberal, and authoritarian political proposals in the second round of the most recent presidential election in December 2021. The circuit of detachment explains how it is that, while most Chileans demand a more egalitarian country, they seek to protect the benefits they have achieved, insist that individual effort is the essential element of personal dignity, and continue to espouse a strong belief in the efficacy of a "strong" exercise of authority.

Acknowledging the importance of the way individuals respond to structural challenges in their everyday experiences has enabled me to reconstruct the ambivalent and somehow paradoxical traits that characterize each of the circuit's components (excessiveness, disenchantment, irritation, and detachment). It has also enabled me to avoid interpreting these processes as mere reflexive responses and to elucidate both actors' agency and the variations in the impact of structural traits as well as individual responses across different social groups. Being from the popular sectors does not only define the impact of structural challenges (the push toward pluriactivity is bigger, to give one example) but also defines the sets of supports they can rely on or mobilize to face these challenges (for example, childcare). The "new start" modality of detachment, which encompasses the idea of building projects and therefore requires long-term planning and plentiful resources, is scarce in these sectors. The "adversarial alternatives" modality concerns younger people. The "refuge" modality of detachment is a more frequent modality in this group, especially for older generations. Similar differences are to be found when considering gender and generational criteria (space limitations reasons precluded me from giving a closer account of all these relevant nuances in this Element).

In view of the above, what is the scope of an interpretation such as the one I have proposed? If the circuit of detachment has occurred in the interaction of specific structural currents and forms of response, must we conclude that the circuit concept is applicable only to the case of Chile or can it be applied to understand other contemporary societies?

The structural currents affecting Chile will not necessarily be the same as ones operating in other societies (though they likely do operate in many other countries). The push for the democratization of social relations, for example, will not have as transformative and disruptive an effect in all societies as it has had in Chile, a society historically characterized by strongly vertical social and political bonds based on lasting and naturalized hierarchies. Although the basic structural challenges can be similar for many societies, each country responds to the challenges in its own way according to its distinctive characteristics and its geopolitical position. Although all societies, and their individuals, must respond to these challenges, not all do so in the same way because the resources, historical inertia, or institutional design from which these responses are structured differ.

Therefore, the most useful way to approach this question may be to empirically test this interpretative framework by applying it to societies that have gone through the so-called neoliberal moment. However, it is worth emphasizing that there are several reasons to believe the circuit of detachment could contribute to the understanding of very different societies. The combined stress of high social demands and meager institutional support is revealed both in the fierce forms of competition and individual affirmation that cross social life, and in the worldwide increased prevalence of emotional discomfort and mental illness. Symptoms such as political disaffection appear in many societies. A general questioning of hierarchies seems to characterize a large number of Western societies, as shown, for example, by the increasingly fractious relationship between citizens and police and the various irritations that this engenders. Mistrust of institutions (science, governments, etc.) is a widespread social trait as well as a relevant factor for the weakening and/or transformation of the notion of truth (McIntyre 2018). Individuals' increasing tendency toward insularity is evidenced in their withdrawal into groups of those like themselves and in the growth of irritated, polarized, and intolerant forms of managing differences (Hetherington and Weiler 2009). The list could go on.

Thus, the scope of the circuit of detachment as an analytical tool must await its testing via the empirical analysis of other cases. As far as Chile's case is concerned, however, some brief remarks can be made on the meaning of the above analysis for Chilean society.

The circuit of detachment can be read as both hopeful and worrying. It is hopeful in that it shows Chile to be a society of individuals who recognize, across the board, the limits and costs for their own lives of the economic, developmental, social, and relational model that has governed them for the past several decades, a society whose members are seeking political and social solutions. It is, at the same time, worrying because the currents that run through Chilean society are very dissimilar: while Chileans aspire to find other ways of living and of building selves, they also feel drawn to inhabit the margins of society or to instrumentalize the situation for their own benefit, whether pragmatically or confrontationally. It is also worrying because, for all their commitment to the ideal of a high-quality communal life, there are many whose deepest desire is to live their lives at a distance from the collective, from their society, its principles, promises, and norms. Finally, it is worrying because the circuit of detachment raises the question of how, in this context of irritation, disenchantment, excessiveness, and detachment, the problem of social and political regulation is to be solved. The social bond in Chile is under pressure to be reconstructed, which produces a high degree of uncertainty regarding the fate of the political bond.

What, then, can be said about the future? At turning points such as the one that Chilean society now faces, social scientists have two obligations. The first is to try to contribute by making sense of events. The second is to recognize our limits because, fortunately, freedom and human agency exist, and societies are complex living entities that do not allow themselves to be confined. In this Element, I have tried to fulfill the first task with humility and I close by acknowledging the second obligation enthusiastically. The outcome remains to be seen. The complex web we call society will determine its own destiny.

Appendix

Investigation 1: Notion of Rights and Relationship with Norms in the Popular and Middle-Class Sectors

This research was developed in two stages, from 2003 to 2004 and from 2005 to 2006. Its objective was to study individuals' relationships with norms and the latter's impact on the orientations of action. As a starting point, the research addressed the question of the role played by law, as a normative ideal (not as positive law), in the regulation of everyday relationships between people, and between them and institutions. In total, twenty-two Conversation-Dramatization Groups (CDGs) were held with between five and eight participants from the middle-class and popular sectors. (CDGs are a combination of conversation groups and dramatization techniques applied to social research and derive from the methodological strategy of participant research.)

This study received support from Oxfam GB. The results of the research were presented in Araujo (2009).

Investigation 2: Individuation Processes in Chilean Society

This research, carried out in collaboration with Danilo Martuccelli, sought to identify the structural social challenges that individuals must confront, how they deal with them, and the type of individuals they are driven to embody when facing them. The fieldwork was carried out between 2007 and 2009. In each case, semi-structured interviews with two interviewers were applied to 96 men and women between 30 and 55 years old, from the middle, upper-middle, and popular sectors of Greater Santiago, Valparaíso, and Concepción.

The research received support from the National Fund for Scientific and Technological Development (Fondecyt), Project 1085006. The results were published in full in Araujo and Martuccelli (2012).

Investigation 3: Authority and Processes of Social Democratization in Chile

This research, carried out between 2011 and 2014, was aimed at identifying forms of the exercise of authority in the context of the pressure for the democratization of social relations in Chile. Thirty-two semi-structured interviews were conducted with men and women from middle sectors and low-resource sectors.

Additionally, twelve CDGs were carried out. In both cases, a requirement was that all those in the sample be between 35 and 55 years of age and have children.

This project was supported by Fondecyt, Project 1110733. A presentation of the full results can be found in Araujo (2016).

Investigation 4: Study of Inequalities and Street Interactions

This study was carried out in 2016 to analyze experiences on the streets of Santiago in the context of the question of inequality and the social bond. Fieldwork was conducted exclusively in Greater Santiago. It focused on five areas: parks, commercial and bohemian neighborhoods, public transport (Metro and buses), avenues, and crowded intersections. Two techniques were used: 1) participant observations carried out by the research team (108) and 2) eight actor-informants were called on to perform participant observations. Each week, each actor-informant was visited by a member of the research team and an in-depth interview was conducted in which their observations were reviewed and discussed based on their field notes. Seven processes were completed, involving a total of twenty-eight interviews. The study was conducted throughout 2016 under the auspices of UNDP-Chile. The results were presented in Araujo (2019b).

Investigation 5: The Work of Individuals and the Constitution of Subjects in Chilean Society: Normative Ideals, Experiences, and Existential Anchors

This study was carried out between 2014 and 2017. It proposed to investigate the work that individuals carry out to face societal challenges, and to reconstruct the ways in which they seek to give themselves consistency, practice, and rules. In-depth interviews were conducted with forty-eight men and women between the ages of 30 and 55 from the middle sectors and popular sectors in the three most populated urban zones of Chile, Santiago, Concepción, and Valparaíso. A semi-directed individual interview technique was used, with two variants: a comprehensive interview and a focused interview based on the use of project-ive material.

This project was supported by Fondecyt, Project 1140055. Partial results were presented in Araujo (2018). Analysis of this material contributed especially to Section 5, Detachment.

Investigation 6: Authority and Power Asymmetries (NUMAAP)

This is not a single study but a research project currently in progress at the research center Millennium Nucleus Center Authority and Asymmetries of

Power (NUMAAP), under my direction. From an interdisciplinary perspective, we investigate the processes by which the mechanisms for managing the exercise of power and authority in Chilean society are reconfigured in three social spheres: work, family, and the public space.

The Center is supported by the ANID-Millennium Scientific Initiative, NCS17_007. Website: www.numaap.cl.

Investigation 7: Transformations of the Relationship between the Public and Parties: A Study from the Perspective of Political Actors

The relationship between institutional politics, society, and individuals was analyzed, with an analytical focus on political actors. The study was carried out between 2017 and 2018, with a qualitative methodological design applied to a sample of forty-five people. Eight individual semi-structured interviews and seven group interviews (a total of thirty-seven participants) were conducted with political actors who participated in the campaign teams for candidates in the 2017 presidential, parliamentary, and regional councilors' elections in Santiago.

This project was funded by the Friedrich Ebert Foundation. The results were presented in Araujo (2017) and Araujo (2019a).

Investigation 8: Problematization of Individualism in South America

Begun in 2018, this is an ongoing study, conducted in collaboration with Danilo Martuccelli, on the trajectory of individualism in South America, focusing on Argentina, Brazil, Chile, Colombia, and Peru. It is an investigation in historical sociology that is organized around the hypothesis that, to understand the fate of individualism in South American societies, one must take account of variations in the tension between a historical mode of agentic individuation and political and legal individualism in its essentially liberal understanding.

This project is supported by ANID, Fondecyt, Project 1180338.

References

Albertus, Michael and Victor Menaldo. 2018. *Authoritarianism and the Elite Origins of Democracy.* Cambridge: Cambridge University Press.

Amable, Bruno. 2011. "Morals and politics in the ideology of neo-liberalism." *Socio- Economic Review* **9**(1): 3–30.

Araujo, Kathya. 2009. *Habitar lo social: usos y abusos en la vida cotidiana en el Chile actual.* Santiago de Chile: LOM Ediciones.

Araujo, Kathya. 2013. "Interactive inequalities and equality in the social bond: a sociological study of equality." Working paper, Series 54, desiguALdades. net, Berlin.

Araujo, Kathya. 2016. *El miedo a los subordinados: una teoría de la autoridad.* Santiago de Chile: LOM Ediciones.

Araujo, Kathya. 2017. "Democracia y transformaciones sociales en Chile: ¿Qué significa actuar democráticamente?" Working paper, Serie Democracia Análisis No. 11, Friedrich-Ebert-Stiftung Chile.

Araujo, Kathya. 2018. "Los anclajes socio-existenciales: el caso de las expectativas de futuro." *Dados* **61**(2): 341–371.

Araujo, Kathya. 2019a. "La política en tiempos de transformación: la relación entre ciudadanía y política institucional desde la perspectiva de los actores políticos." Working paper, Serie Democracia Análisis No. 3, Friederich-Ebert-Stiftung Chile. Available at http://library.fes.de/pdf-files/bueros/chile/15387.pdf [last accessed December 19, 2021].

Araujo, Kathya, ed. 2019b. *Las Calles: un estudio sobre Santiago de Chile.* Santiago de Chile: LOM Ediciones.

Araujo, Kathya and Danilo Martuccelli. 2012. *Desafíos comunes: la sociedad chilena y sus individuos.* 2 vols. Santiago de Chile: LOM Ediciones.

Araujo, Kathya and Danilo Martuccelli. 2014. "Beyond institutional individualism: agentic individualism and the individuation process in Chilean society." *Current Sociology* **62**(1): 24–40.

Arce, Moises and Paul Bellinger. 2007. "Low-intensity democracy revisited: the effects of economic liberalization on political activity in Latin America." *World Politics* **60**(1): 97–121.

Ariztía, Tomás. 2004. "Nueva Pobreza, patrimonio y sociedad de consumo." *Revista CIS* **4**: 46–53.

Bargsted, Matías and Nicolás Somma. 2018. "La cultura política: diagnóstico y evolución." In Huneeus, P. and O. Avendaño (eds.), *El sistema político de Chile.* Santiago: LOM Ediciones, pp. 193–224.

Barozet, Emmanuelle. 2006. "El valor histórico del pituto: clase media, integración y diferenciación social en Chile." *Revista de Sociología* **20**: 69–96.

Bastías, Gabriel, Paula Bedregal, Juan Carlos Ferrer, Mariana Filgueias, Mathias Klapp, and Cristobal Tello. 2020. *Propuestas para desconfinar la espera en la salud pública. Temas de la Agenda Pública, No. 132.* Santiago: Centro de Políticas Públicas PUC.

Beck, Ulrich. 1992. *Risk Society: Towards a New Modernity.* London: SAGE.

Bell, Daniel. 1976. *The Cultural Contradictions of Capitalism.* New York: Basic Books.

Bengoa, José. 1996. *La comunidad perdida.* Santiago de Chile: SUR Ediciones.

Bouvier, Pierre. 2005. *Le lien social.* Paris: Gallimard.

Brinks, M. Daniel, Steven Levitsky, and María Victoria Murillo. 2019. *Understanding Institutional Weakness: Power and Design in Latin American Institutions.* Cambridge: Cambridge University Press.

Bröckling, Ulrich. 2017. *Gute Hirten führen sanft.* Frankfurt am Main: Suhrkamp.

Brunner, José Joaquín. 1992. *América Latina: cultura y modernidad.* Mexico City: Grijalbo.

Buchanan, James. 1986. *Liberty, Market and State: Political Economy in the 1980s.* Brighton: Wheatsheaf Books.

Büchi, Hernán. 2008. *La transformación económica de Chile: el modelo del progreso.* Santiago de Chile: Aguilar Ediciones.

CNDU (Consejo Nacional de Desarrollo Urbano). 2020. "Sistema de Indicadores y estándares de desarrollo urbano." Available at http://siedu.ine.cl/tiempo_DE_16.html# [last accessed March 11, 2021].

Collier, Simon and William Sater. 1999. *A History of Chile 1808–1994.* Cambridge: Cambridge University Press.

Corporación Latinobarómetro. 2020. "Informe Chile." Available at https://bit.ly/3bmp2HX [last accessed March 20, 2021].

Cox, Loreto, Andrés Hernando, and Andrea Rebolledo. 2018. "Una evaluación de la educación superior: la mirada de los estudiantes." *Estudios Públicos* **150**: 7–74.

Dagnino, Evelina, Alberto Olivera, and Aldo Panfichi, coordinators. 2006. *La disputa por la construcción democrática en América Latina.* Mexico City: Fondo de Cultura Económica, Centro de Investigaciones y Estudios Superiores en Antropología Social, Universidad Veracruzana.

Dahrendorf, Ralf. 1985. *Law and Order.* London: Steven & Sons.

Dardot, Pierre and Christian Laval. 2009. *La nouvelle raison du monde: essai sur la société néolibérale.* Paris: La Découverte.

Davies, William. 2014. *The Limits of Neoliberalism: Authority, Sovereignty and the Logic of Competition*. London: SAGE.

Domingues, José Mauricio. 2009. *La modernidad contemporánea en América Latina*. Buenos Aires: Siglo XXI Editores.

Drake, Paul and Ivan Jaksic, eds. 2002. *El modelo chileno: democracia y desarrollo en los noventa*. Santiago: LOM Ediciones.

Durán, Gonzalo and Marco Kremerman. 2020. "Los Verdaderos Sueldos de Chile: Panorama actual del Valor de la Fuerza de Trabajo usando la Encuesta Suplementaria de Ingresos ESI (2019)." Working paper, Serie Salarios y Desigualdad Fundación Sol. Available at https://bit.ly/3ykIi1J [last accessed March 20, 2021].

Durkheim, Émile. 1979. *Suicide: A Study in Sociology*. New York: The Free Press.

Elias, Norbert. 2000. *The Civilizing Process: Sociogenetic and Psychogenetic Investigations*. Oxford: Blackwell Publishing.

Errázuriz, Paula, Camila Valdés, Paul Vöhringer, and Esteban Calvo. 2015. "Mental health financing in Chile: a pending debate." *Revista médica de Chile* **143**(9): 1179–1186.

Espinoza, Vicente, Emmanuelle Barozet, and María Luisa Méndez. 2013. "Estratificación y movilidad social bajo un modelo neoliberal: el caso de Chile." *Lavboratorio* **14**(25): 169–191.

FONASA (Fondo Nacional de Salud). 2018. "Boletín estadístico 2017–2018." Available at www.fonasa.cl/sites/fonasa/adjuntos/boletin_estadistico_20172018 [last accessed December 16, 2021].

Garretón, Manuel Antonio. 2000. *La sociedad en que vivi(re)mos*. Santiago de Chile: LOM Ediciones.

Garretón, Manuel Antonio. 2012. *Neoliberalismo corregido y progresismo limitado: los gobiernos de la Concertación en Chile 1990–2010*. Santiago de Chile: Arcis/CLACSO.

Gobierno de Chile. 2018. *Norma general administrativa sobre agresiones al personal de atención en establecimiento de salud*. Available at https://bit.ly/3A8aFRV [last accessed March 5, 2021].

Goffman, Erving. 1959. *The Presentation of Self in Everyday Life*. New York: Doubleday.

Gonzáles, Ricardo. 2017. *¿Malestar en Chile? Informe Encuesta CEP 2016*. Santiago de Chile: Centro de Estudios Públicos.

Guzmán, Eugenio and Marcel Oppliger. 2012. *El malestar de Chile: ¿teoría o diagnóstico?* Santiago de Chile: RIL Editores.

Han, Clara. 2012. *Life in Debt: Times of Care and Violence in Neoliberal Chile*. Berkeley: University of California Press.

Harvey, David. 2005. *A Brief History of Neoliberalism*. Oxford: Oxford University Press.

Hetherington, J. Marc and Jonathan D. Weiler. 2009. *Authoritarianism and Polarization in American Politics*. Cambridge: Cambridge University Press.

Hirschman, Albert. 1970. *Exit, Voice and Loyalty: Responses to Decline of Firms, Organizations and State*. Cambridge, MA: Harvard University Press.

Hunneus, Carlos. 2003. *Chile: un país dividido*. Santiago: Catalonia.

INE (Instituto Nacional de Estadísticas). 1988. *Encuesta de presupuestos familiares (IV)*. Available at https://bit.ly/3QQcjNS [last accessed March 9, 2021].

INE (Instituto Nacional de Estadísticas). 2017. *Encuesta de Presupuestos Familiares (VIII)*. Available at https://bit.ly/3QQbqow [last accessed March 9, 2021].

INJUV (Instituto Nacional de la Juventud). 2020. *Sondeo: endeudamiento juvenil y educación financiera*. Available at https://bit.ly/3A4NUhH [last accessed March 23, 2021].

Innerarity, Daniel. 2020. *Una teoría de la democracia compleja*. Barcelona: Galaxia Gutenberg.

Joignant, Alfredo, Matías Garretón, Nicolás Somma, and Tomás Campos, eds. 2020. *Informe Anual Observatorio de Conflictos 2020*. Santiago, Chile: COES. Available at https://bit.ly/3A5R6K2 [last accessed March 18, 2021].

Julián, Dasten. 2018. Precariedad laboral y repertorios sindicales en el neoliberalismo: cambios en la politización del trabajo en Chile. *Psicoperspectivas* [online] **17**(1). Available at https://doi.org/10.5027/psicoperspectivas-vol17-issue1-fulltext-947 [last accessed November 21, 2019].

Khan, Shamus. 2011. *Privilege: The Making of an Adolescent Elite at St. Paul's School*. Princeton, NJ: Princeton University Press.

Kurtz, Markus. 2004. "The dilemmas of democracy in the open economy: lessons from Latin America." *World Politics* **56**(2): 262–302.

Larraín, Jorge. 2001. *La identidad chilena*. Santiago de Chile: LOM Ediciones.

Lechner, Norbert. 1990. *Los patios interiores de la democracia: subjetividad y política*. Santiago de Chile: Fondo de Cultura Económica.

Lechner, Norbert. 2006. *Obras escogidas*, tomo 1. Santiago de Chile: LOM Ediciones.

Levitsky, Steven and Daniel Ziblatt. 2018. *How Democracies Die*. New York: Crown.

Luna, Juan Pablo. 2017. *En vez del optimismo: crisis de la representación política en el Chile actual*. Santiago de Chile: Catalonia.

Martuccelli, Danilo. 2006. *Forgé par l'épreuve*. Paris: Armand Colin.

Martuccelli, Danilo. 2015. *Lima y sus Arenas*. Lima: Cauces editores.

Martuccelli, Danilo. 2021. *La sociedad desformal*. São Paulo: Edicões Plataforma Democratica.

Martuccelli, Danilo and François de Singly. 2018. *L'individue et ses sociologies*. Paris: Armand Colin.

Mayol, Alberto. 2013. *El derrumbe del modelo: la crisis de la economía de mercado en el Chile contemporáneo*. Santiago de Chile: LOM Ediciones.

Mayol, Alberto, Carla Azócar, and Carlos Azócar. 2013. *El Chile Profundo: modelos culturales de la desigualdad y sus resistencias*. Santiago de Chile: Liberalia Ediciones.

McIntyre, Lee. 2018. *Post-Truth*. Boston, MA: The MIT Press.

Merton Robert. 1938. "Social structure and anomie." *American Sociological Review* **3**(5): 672–682.

Metro de Santiago. 2007. *Memoria anual metro S.A. '07*. Available at www.metrosantiago.cl/files/documentos/anuario.pdf [last accessed August 16, 2018].

Metro de Santiago. 2015. *Memoria anual 2015*. Available at www.metrosantiago.cl/files/documentos/memoria2015/memoria-anual-2015.pdf [last accessed August 16, 2018].

MINDES (Ministerio de Desarrollo Social y Familia). 2020. *Evolución de la pobreza 1990–2017: ¿Cómo ha cambiado Chile?* Available at https://bit.ly/3btFpTe [last accessed March 10, 2021].

MINEDUC (Ministerio de Educación). 2020. *Visualización gráfica de matrículas*. Available at https://bit.ly/3xWoqk3 [last accessed March 11, 2021].

MINEDUC (Ministerio de Educación). 2021. *Apuntes N° 12 Variación de la Matrícula 2020*. Available at https://centroestudios.mineduc.cl/publicaciones-ce/minutas/ [last accessed April 3, 2022].

Molina, Raúl. 2020. *Hablan los muros: grafitis de la rebelión social de octubre de 2019*. Santiago de Chile: LOM Ediciones.

Morales, Liliana and Álvaro Yáñez. 2006. "Créditos de consumo bancarios: evolución reciente 1997–2005." Serie técnica de Estudios, 03. Superintendencia de Bancos e Instituciones Financieras. Santiago de Chile: SBIF.

Moulian, Tomás. 1997. *Chile, anatomía de un mito*. Santiago de Chile: LOM Ediciones.

Moulian, Tomás. 1998. *El consumo me consume*. Santiago de Chile: LOM Ediciones.

Mouriaux, Marie-Françoise. 2006. "La qualité de l'emploi au prisme de la pluriactivité." In Centre d'études de l'emploi, *La qualité de l'emploi* [online], Paris, La Découverte, pp. 54–63. Available at www.cairn.info/la-qualite-de-l-emploi–9782707148933-page-54.htm [last accessed July 26, 2021].

OECD (Organisation for Economic Co-operation and Development). 2019. *Health at a Glance 2019: OECD Indicators.* Available at https://bit.ly/3nerFhV [last accessed March 10, 2021].

OECD (Organisation for Economic Co-operation and Development). 2020. *Education at a Glance: OECD Indicators.* Paris: OECD Publications.

Ordóñez, Felix and Ignacio Silva. 2019. "Estructura productiva y dificultades para el crecimiento de largo plazo en Chile." *Revista Economía y Desafíos del Desarrollo* [online] **1**(4): 2–30. Available at www.unsam.edu.ar/escuelas/economia/revistaedd/2c_n4/ [last accessed November 3, 2021].

Paugam, Serge. 2017. *Vivre ensemble dans un monde incertain.* Paris: Éditions de l'Aube.

Penaglia, Francesco and Silvania Mejías. 2019. El conflicto estudiantil chileno y sus efectos políticos. *Revista Polis México*, **15**(2). https://doi.org/10.24275/uam/izt/dcsh/polis/2019v15n2/penaglia.

Pérez-Ahumada, Pablo. 2018. "Clases sociales, sectores económicos y cambios en la estructura social chilena entre 1992 y 2013." *Revista de la CEPAL* **126**: 171–192.

Pinedo, Javier. 1997. "Chile a fines del siglo XX: entre la modernidad, la modernización y la identidad." *Revista Universum* **12**: 1–40.

PNUD (Programa de Naciones Unidas para el Desarrollo). 1998. *Informe de Desarrollo Humano en Chile: las paradojas de la modernización.* Santiago de Chile: PNUD.

PNUD (Programa de Naciones Unidas para el Desarrollo). 2002. *Informe de Desarrollo Humano en Chile: nosotros los chilenos: un desafío cultural.* Santiago de Chile: PNUD.

PNUD (Programa de Naciones Unidas para el Desarrollo). 2015. *Desarrollo Humano en Chile: los tiempos de la politización.* Santiago de Chile: PNUD.

PNUD (Programa de Naciones Unidas para el Desarrollo). 2017. *Desiguales: orígenes, cambios y desafíos de la brecha social en Chile.* Santiago de Chile: PNUD.

PUC (Pontificia Universidad Católica de Chile). 2019. *Encuesta Nacional Bicentenario: movilidad social.* Available at https://bit.ly/39Q3yD8 [last accessed March 9, 2021].

Raczynski, Dagmar. 1994. "Políticas sociales y programas de combate a la pobreza en Chile: balances y desafíos." *Colección Estudios CIEPLAN* **39**.

Ramos, Claudio. 2009. *La transformación de la empresa chilena.* Santiago de Chile: Universidad Alberto Hurtado.

Ramos, Joseph. 2004. "Vulnerables." In Ramos, J. (ed.), *Cómo ha cambiado la vida de los chilenos ... Análisis comparativo de las condiciones de vida en los hogares con menos bienestar socioeconómico (Censos 1992–2002).* Santiago de Chile: INE, pp. 25–44.

Rancière, Jacques. 1995. *On the Shores of Politics.* London: Verso.

Rasse, Alejandra. 2019. *La crisis de la vivienda: entre el derecho social y la oferta inmobiliaria.* In Araujo, K. (ed.), *Hilos tensados: para leer el octubre chileno.* Santiago de Chile: Editorial USACH Colección IDEA, pp. 107–125.

Roberts, Kenneth. 2008. "The mobilization of opposition to economic liberalization." *Annual Review of Political Science* 11: 327–349.

Ruiz, Carlos. 2020. *Octubre chileno: la irrupción de un nuevo pueblo.* Santiago de Chile: Taurus.

Ruiz, Carlos and Giorgio Boccardo. 2015. *Los chilenos bajo el neoliberalismo.* Santiago de Chile: Nodo XXI/El desconcierto.

Salazar, Gabriel and Julio Pinto. 1999. *Historia contemporánea de Chile, tomo 1: estado, legitimidad, ciudadanía.* Santiago: LOM.

Sandel, Michael. 2020. *Tyranny of Merit: What's Become of the Common Good?* New York: Farrar, Straus and Giroux.

Schneider, Ben. 2013. *Hierarchical Capitalism in Latin America.* Cambridge: Cambridge University Press.

Somma, Nicolás. 2017. "Discontent, collective protest, and social movements in Chile." In Joignant, Alfredo, Mauricio Morales, and Claudio Fuentes (eds.), *Malaise in Representation in Latin American Countries: Chile, Argentina, and Uruguay.* New York: Palgrave Macmillan, pp. 47–68.

Soto, Álvaro and Carla Fardella. 2019. "Del yo al nosotros: el emplazamiento colectivo a las subjetividades neoliberales." In Araujo, K. (ed.) *Hilos tensados: para leer el octubre chileno.* Santiago: Colección IDEA/Editorial USACH, pp. 243–270.

Stecher, Antonio and Vicente Sisto. 2019. "Trabajo y precarización laboral en el Chile neoliberal: apuntes para comprender el estallido social de octubre de 2019." In Araujo, K. (ed.), *Hilos tensados: para leer el octubre chileno.* Santiago: Colección IDEA/Editorial USACH, pp. 37–82.

Stecher, Antonio, Lorena Godoy, and Antonio Aravena. 2020. "Sindicalismo y vida cotidiana en el Retail: experiencias de dirigentes de base en Chile." *Psicoperspectivas* 19(3): 1–11.

Streeck Wolfgang. 2011. "The crises of democratic capitalism." *New Left Review* 71: 5–29.

SUBTEL (Subsecretaría de Telecomunicaciones). 2016. *VII Encuesta de Acceso y Usos de Internet.* Available at https://bit.ly/3xQzZt3 [last accessed March 26, 2021].

Tilly Charles. 2005. *Identity, Boundaries and Social Ties.* Boulder, CO: Paradigm Publishers.

Tirachini, Alejandro, David Hensher, and John Rose. 2013. "Seis pasajeros por metro cuadrado: efectos del hacinamiento en la oferta de transporte público, el bienestar de los usuarios y la estimación de demanda." Paper presented at Congreso Chileno de Ingeniería de Transporte [online] (16). Available at https://revistas.uchile.cl/index.php/CIT/article/view/28402/30097 [last accessed August 20, 2018].

Tironi, Eugenio. 1999. *La irrupción de las masas y el malestar de las elites.* Santiago de Chile: Grijalbo.

Valdés, Juan Gabriel. 1995. *Pinochet's Economists: The Chicago School in Chile.* Cambridge: Cambridge University Press.

Vargas, Virginia. 2008. *Feminismos en América Latina: su aporte a la política y a la democracia.* Lima: UNMSM/Centro Flora Tristán/Programa Democracia y Transformación Global.

Venegas, Sebastián. 2017. "Significados de la Prueba Social del Trabajo en Trabajadores por Cuenta Propia: ideales, experiencias y soportes." Unpublished Masters dissertation, Universidad Alberto Hurtado.

Vergara, Ana, Paulina Chávez, and Enrique Vergara. 2010. "Televidencia y vida cotidiana de la infancia." *Revista Polis* **9**(26): 371–396.

WID (World Inequality Database). 2019. "Top 10% national income share." Available at https://bit.ly/3A3bRpH [last accessed January 30, 2021].

Acknowledgments

I gratefully acknowledge the support given by the Desarrollo de Chile (ANID) through the Fondecyt Project 1180338 and the Millennium Initiative Program NCS17-007.

Cambridge Elements ☰

Politics and Society in Latin America

Maria Victoria Murillo
Columbia University

Maria Victoria Murillo is Professor of Political Science and International Affairs at Columbia University. She is the author of *Political Competition, Partisanship, and Policymaking in the Reform of Latin American Public Utilities* (Cambridge, 2009). She is also editor of *Carreras Magisteriales, Desempeño Educativo y Sindicatos de Maestros en América Latina* (2003), and co-editor of *Argentine Democracy: The Politics of Institutional Weakness* (2005). She has published in edited volumes as well as in the *American Journal of Political Science, World Politics*, and *Comparative Political Studies*, among others.

Tulia G. Falleti
University of Pennsylvania

Tulia G. Falleti is the Class of 1965 Endowed Term Professor of Political Science, Director of the Latin American and Latino Studies Program, and Senior Fellow of the Leonard Davis Institute for Health Economics at the University of Pennsylvania. She received her BA in Sociology from the Universidad de Buenos Aires and her Ph.D. in Political Science from Northwestern University. Falleti is the author of *Decentralization and Subnational Politics in Latin America* (Cambridge University Press, 2010), which earned the Donna Lee Van Cott Award for best book on political institutions from the Latin American Studies Association, and with Santiago Cunial of *Participation in Social Policy: Public Health in Comparative Perspective* (Cambridge University Press, 2018). She is co-editor, with Orfeo Fioretos and Adam Sheingate, of *The Oxford Handbook of Historical Institutionalism* (Oxford University Press, 2016), among other edited books. Her articles on decentralization, federalism, authoritarianism, and qualitative methods have appeared in edited volumes and journals such as the *American Political Science Review, Comparative Political Studies, Publius, Studies in Comparative International Development*, and *Qualitative Sociology*, among others.

Juan Pablo Luna
The Pontifical Catholic University of Chile

Juan Pablo Luna is Professor of Political Science at The Pontifical Catholic University of Chile. He received his BA in Applied Social Sciences from the UCUDAL (Uruguay) and his PhD in Political Science from the University of North Carolina at Chapel Hill. He is the author of *Segmented Representation: Political Party Strategies in Unequal Democracies* (Oxford University Press, 2014), and has co-authored *Latin American Party Systems* (Cambridge University Press, 2010). In 2014, along with Cristobal Rovira, he co-edited *The Resilience of the Latin American Right* (Johns Hopkins University). His work on political representation, state capacity, and organized crime has appeared in the following journals: *Comparative Political Studies, Revista de Ciencia Política*, the *Journal of Latin American Studies, Latin American Politics and Society, Studies in Comparative International Development, Política y Gobierno, Democratization, Perfiles Latinoamericanos*, and the *Journal of Democracy*.

Andrew Schrank
Brown University

Andrew Schrank is the Olive C. Watson Professor of Sociology and International & Public Affairs at Brown University. His articles on business, labor, and the state in Latin America have appeared in the *American Journal of Sociology, Comparative Politics, Comparative Political Studies, Latin American Politics & Society, Social Forces*, and *World Development*, among other journals, and his co-authored book, *Root-Cause Regulation: Labor Inspection in Europe and the Americas*, is forthcoming at Harvard University Press.

About the Series

Latin American politics and society are at a crossroads, simultaneously confronting serious challenges and remarkable opportunities that are likely to be shaped by formal institutions and informal practices alike. The Elements series on Politics and Society in Latin America offers multidisciplinary and methodologically pluralist contributions on the most important topics and problems confronted by the region.

Cambridge Elements ≡

Politics and Society in Latin America